AUGUST 2022

AN ANTHOLOGY OF ARTICLES

BRAIN BOOSTER ARTICLES

Contents

Preface

"Start writing, no matter what. The water does not flow until the faucet is turned on".

- Louis L'Amour

This book is a bouquet of articles contributed by students, professors and academicians. Hundreds of students and professors are contributing their work to Brain Booster Articles, we are here to provide ample information about Law and Contemporary issues. Our aim is to provide a platform for today's generation to express their views and ideas on law and contemporary law.

CHAPTER ONE

ADULTERY AND LAW: ANALYSIS

Author: Sabari K S, IV year of B.A.,LL.B.(Hons.) from School of excellence in law, TNDALU, Chennai.

ABSTRACT

This article aims to provide an analysis of the present legal and social status of adultery in India. Through this, the position of adultery before and after decriminalization is analysed. The position of adultery in India and other countries is also taken into analysis. Relevant important landmark cases and their judgments related to adultery are discussed. This article provides an insight into adultery in India.

INTRODUCTION

Adultery is a voluntary sexual activity of a spouse and an individual who is not a spouse of him/her. Simply, it is also known as a consensual extramarital relationship. It is considered objectionable on social, religious, moral, and previously on legal grounds too. Adultery has its origin from a Latin word called 'adulterium', meaning corrupt.

According to Section 497[1] of IPC, 1860, four essentials of adultery are

- Sexual intercourse
- With a person who is the wife of another man
- Without the consent or connivance of that man
- Not amounting to rape

The punishment was the imprisonment of 5 years or fine or both. A wife was not punished as an abettor.

ANALYSIS ON LAW IN RELATION TO ADULTERY

Yusuf Aziz vs State of Bombay[2]

In this case, the petitioner questioned the validity of Section 497, IPC as it was violative of Articles 14, 15 of the Constitution of India. The Court held that they are not violative as the immunity to women was not violative as the immunity to a woman was not discriminatory but valid points put forth by the petitioner were taken up in the Joseph Shine case. The point was that "Adultery can only be committed by man because women are not punished as an abettor". This view was rejected in the 2018 landmark case.

Sowmitri Vishnu vs. Union of India[3]

Section 497 was challenged as violative of Articles 14, 15, and 21. But the court held that it was not violative. Because not allowing spouses to prosecute against each other law offers them a chance to make up. Also. women are considered to be a victim of man, who has unstoppable charm.

The apex court is of the stand that it is the policy of the law not to punish women for adultery and policies could not be questioned. Adultery is considered to be an offense against a matrimonial home. [4]

Why women were not punished for adultery?

During earlier days when the law was enacted polygamy was deep-rooted in society. So, women shared their husbands with other wives and extramarital affairs. Therefore, women were considered victims, who could give themselves up to any person who offered them affection and love. So, the provision was made accordingly to restrict men from having sexual relations with wives of other men and at the same time to restrict their relations with an unmarried woman alone.

Joseph Shine vs Union of India[5]

In 2018 Section 497 of IPC was struck down in this case by 5 Judges comprising of Justice Deepak Misra, Justice DY Chandrachud, and others. Further, it was held that if any aggrieved spouse commits suicide, based on the evidence could be treated as an abetment to suicide attracting Section 306 of IPC. Also, it is continued to be treated as a valid ground for divorce.

It was decriminalized because women were considered property of men, also equality was violated. These issues along with analysis of the modern era contributed to striking down. It was a landmark case.

Rights Reassured after Decriminalising

- Right to Equality provided by Article 14 of the constitution
- Right against discrimination as provided under Article 15 of the Constitution.

- The right to sexual expression is guaranteed as a right to freedom of speech and expression under Article 19.
- State interference in personal matters of an individual.

Ground for Divorce

According to Hindu Marriage Act, 1955 – Section 13(1): Any voluntary sexual intercourse with a person who is not a spouse, is a ground for divorce. Section 10 defines adultery as a ground for judicial separation. Supreme Court confirmed that adultery is a ground for divorce, though not a criminal offense. Special Marriage Act, 1954 stated that if a person had any sexual activity outside marital relation, it is a valid ground for divorce.Section 22 of the Indian Divorce Act made provisions of Judicial Separation on the ground of adultery.

Religious, Moral, and Ethical Views

In Hinduism, marriage is a relationship that is sacramental and continues for seven consequent births. So, it is sacramental needing at most loyalty. In Islam, adultery is treated as a Zina (sin). For those punishments are prescribed by God. Adulterers are to be stoned to death, accordingly.

In Christianity adultery is a sin deserving death. In Buddhism, adultery is a sin leading to suffering. The Judaist view is that there is a provision for the death penalty for adulterers.

Morally, sexual infidelity is prima facie wrong because it involves promise-breaking. Ethically also adultery is wrong. This is because cheating is not an ethical practice. Especially cheating in sex and other matters violates ethical reciprocity and fair nature.

Therefore, adultery is wrong from religious, moral, and ethical views.

ADULTERY IN VARIOUS COUNTRIES

United Kingdom

In the UK, the legal position regarding adultery is similar to that of India's present legal position. It is decriminalized there. But it is a ground for divorce in the UK for both spouses. Spouses will not be allowed to use adultery as a ground for divorce if both were living together as a couple for six months after the sexual act outside marriage was known.

However, the way through which this was made not a criminal offense differs. In India, it was through the Joseph Shine case, whereas in the UK through a private member bill in Matrimonial Causes Act, 1923. In Taiwan, adultery is punished by up to one year in prison (imprisonment).

Indonesia

In adultery law, Indonesia is a little strict as it considers it a crime. But actually, Indonesia is drafting laws that criminalize all sexual activity that is consensual outside wedlock.

United States of America

In the USA, 21 states, adultery is considered to be illegal. But the provision is not discriminatory, unlike India's previous position. Both men and women can sue each other for adultery. Anyways, according to a BBC report, most Americas do not consider it to be a crime. Apart from these 21 states, in other states, it is either not a crime or applies only to a married woman. Certain states are considering their position to decriminalize adultery laws.

Islamic States

Adultery is prohibited in Muslim law, so it is a criminal offense in countries such as Iran, Saudi Arabia, Afghanistan, Pakistan, Bangladesh, and Somalia.

South Korea

In 2015, Supreme Court struck down adultery in a case in which a man got two years imprisonment for adultery. The court held that the law violating self-determination as well as privacy.

More than 60 countries around the world had done away with laws that criminalized adultery.

<u>CONCLUSION</u>

In analysing adultery in this present modern era from a development viewpoint also concerning the position in other countries, the striking down of discriminatory Section 497 is appropriate. The judgment given by the Apex Court in Joseph Shine vs Union of India is a landmark that will stand high, whenever any dispute in this regard pops up. If this was not done, our country would have remained legally backward with such a biased and disputed provision of Section 497. Also, by keeping it as a ground for divorce, the apex court has acknowledged the need for an aggrieved spouse.

The decriminalization of Section 497 in a way helped in improving the status of women. This reassured equality. Also, in another point of view, even a male's position has improved because only he was punished for a consensual act. Therefore, this decriminalization is positively beneficial from both a social and legal perspective.

CHAPTER TWO

ANTI- EFFECTS OF HORSE TRADING

Author: Neha Kachhawaha, IV year of B.B.A.,LL.B. from B.M. Law College

ABSTRACT

A concept which has been developed since back in 19th century in western countries, where people use to buy and sell horses, also termed as 'horse dealing'. It can also be defined as negotiation which is accompanied by smart bargaining and reciprocal concessions. Lately, this term was widely used in western countries in the arena of their political system, from where it came out and prompted many other political systems, where India was one of them. The expression was coined in 1960s in Haryana where it witnessed excessive horse trading and counter horse trading, which took place in many areas of the state. This event came out to be one of the major reasons behind the term 'Aaya Ram Gaya Ram' and also resulting in increased number of occasions where members of the parties were withdrawing themselves in the lure of their monetary purpose. Because of this, it left a great impact on the economic condition of India. This led to the enactment of Defection Law which was initiated by the Indian Congress which was the ruling party at that point of time. Since then, there has been major amendments in the act, which has barred the members to leave the party without 2/3rd of its majority. One on the most important aim of this Act was to bring a political stability in the country through such limitations. But apparently, it looks like it had turned out to be something contradictory in this contemporary scenario, where the members and the leaders of politically ruling parties are more concerned about how can they bring their rival down or take monetary benefitson account of their powers. Least of them are actually concerned about the GDP, per capita income, poverty, hunger, public's health, safety and education etc... and to make these issues as a central concern of every political party's aim, we need more strong reforms and modifications in not only laws of defection but in every other arena concerned to it.

KEYWORDS: Defection, Party, Members, Disqualification, Violation

<u>INTRODUCTION</u>

This concept is not novel but something which is been practiced since the gilded agean era which extended from 1870 to 1900, this era was period of rapid economic growth both for northern and western United States. The term came into practice around 1820 which simply means buying and selling of horses, also defined as 'horse dealing'. Kabul was one of the key hubs for horse trading.

This term is nowadays in practice in the arena of politics, where it has been developed and has come to refer explicitly to political vote trading which in most common sense known as logrolling. The term may differ from country to country but the purpose is the same. According to Macmillan English Dictionary, it has been defined as dishonest discussions between people who are trying to reach to an agreement.

This term at some point of time was not considered effective and lawful in many political systems for the reason that many political leaders and members of different parties used it for deceiving the voters for making them believe in something which wasn't true especially for personal gains.

When ex-President of United States for Theodore Roosevelt was criticized during his political career when he stood for presidential ballots where he made political alliances with other parties and was attacked by the media reporters. After obtaining the post of president he remarked: "In politics, we have to do a great many things that we ought not to do". Another US president William Jefferson "Bill" Clinton was also slated by the US media for initiating rounds of deal-making in garnering support for the house vote on the North American Free Trade Agreement.[1]

The paradigm of Ramsay Mac Donald is one of the cases occurred in United Kingdom where he was terminated from the post of leader of the Labour Party in August 1931 and just after that he founded a National Government. He didn't resign his seat but weeks after his crossing the floor there was a general election, where he was re-elected. Further many well-known Parliamentary figures like Sir John Simon, Snowdown, Thomas and Sankey during the passé of severe economic and financial crisis were forced to leave their parties. After stepping down they formed groups as Liberal Nationals, National Labour etc. even after their fault critics acknowledged their action as an inspiration which rescued Britain from serious crisis. [2]

Since after independence India has become ademocratic country where the leaders are representatives who are being elected through the majority votes of the citizens. As a result, when a political party wins the election and form its governments, they not only represent the country but also stand in for the ideologies which are been chosen by the civic at large. Citizens place there whole and sole trust in the government, on the core of theirpromises and ideologies. But the leaders get lured by the opposition party's offers before completion of their tenure, creating problem of political defection which poses challenging barrier before the democracy.

<u>INDIAN PERSPECT</u>

The first move where these front-runners were placed near to the ground wasthrough introduction of Anti-Defection Bill proposed by Rajiv Gandhi which was passed overwhelmingly by both the houses, was inserted in the 10th schedule of the Constitution of India via 52nd Constitutional Amendment Act (1985, March 18), which would cancel their membership if they are found embracing the political defection for their personal gains in the concerned house of legislature including state legislatures.

Moreover, 91st Constitutional Amendment Act, 2003 which came into force on 7th July, 2004. This restricted the overall number of ministers in both Central Council of Ministers and State Council who shall not exceed beyond the 15% of respective House's and Assembly's total strength.

The word "defection" is derived from the Latin word "defection" which simply means quitting and shifting one's loyalties from one political party to another. Such defection is rampant in almost every democratic management around the world.

The 10thSchedule has been designed with theaim to prevent the members from violating the mandate of the party in the allure of office or material benefits or for any other reason and if they still perform any such conduct, he will lose the membership from the said assembly. The decision of disqualification arising out of defection shall be given by the presiding officer of the concerned House.

Is such decision given by the presiding officer subject to judicial review or not? Initially when the Act was framed there was no such provision mentioning judicial review and the decision of presiding officer was final and could not be question by the judiciary. But the Supreme Court held in Dr. Kashinath G. Jalmi and Anr. vs Speaker and Ors.[3] that the Speaker/ Chairman has no authority of review under the Tenth Schedule and that the Speaker order is finally subject to judicial review, as held in KihotoHollohan's case[4].

This schedule has been drafted not only to prevent such violations but also to protect the democratic repute and status of the nation at the intercontinental pedestal. It also aims to guard and defend the fundamental right of voting of the citizens of the nation, who cast their valuable vote to the political parties with an intention to see their nationflourish and strengthen like other developed nations.

There are few grounds mentioned under the 10th Schedule where on the grounds of defection the MPs and MLAs can be disqualified:

- If he voluntarily gives up his membership from the political party.
- If he votes in contradiction of the directions issued by his political party.
- If he joins any other party.
- If the nominated member joins the other party after the end of 6 months.
- If the Speaker or the Chairman gives his final decision on disqualification.

There is imperishable history of defection in India. Dating back the period of pre-independence when Shyam Lal Nehru, National Legislature's member changed his alliances from Congress Party to British India. Then, in year 1937, a member of Legislative Assembly of U.P. shifted from the Muslim League to join the Congress. There is very popular Indian term which is used for political horse trading i.e., "Aaya Ram Gaya Ram" which was coined in 1967 by Gaya Lal, member of the Legislative Assembly of Haryana. He joined Indian National Congress, where he changed his political alliance three times in a single day.

In recent years there has been number of incidents of horse trading that were faced by Indian politics, which resulted in fall and rise in government in many different states of the nation. Madhya Pradesh faced an intense political uproar in 2020, which collapsed the Congress government and upsurged the BJP government. In 2018 election Congress was the single party who won 114 seats with the help of independent MLAs and also MLAs of Bahujan Samaj Party and Samajwadi Party and formed their government in the state. Since the formation of the government the tension intensified between chief minister Kamal Nath and JyotiradityaScindiawho is known to be one of the most popular youth leaders. This resulted in resignation of Scindia from Congress on 10 March,2020.

It was reported that before giving the resignation letter to the Congress President, Sonia Gandhi, Scindia met Prime Minister Narendra Modi and Union Home Minister Amit Shah. In the wake of Scindia's resignation, 22 other Congress MLAs resigned with him too and joined BJP the very next day. Many Congress leaders blasted over the saffron party, saying BJP was "shamelessly executing horse-trading". In result of which Supreme Court on March 19, 2020 ordered to conduct floor test in MP Legislative Assembly, where Kamal Nath's government failed to pass the test and ended and it was replaced by BJP government headed by Shivraj Singh Chouhan.

Similar incident took place in Maharashtra Assembly elections in 2019, where BJP the largest party with 105 seats fails when its ally Shiv Sena who won 56 seats, pulled back its alliance with BJP mainly over who will become the chief minister and form a coalition government with NCP and Congress who won 54 and 44 seats respectively. [5]

<u>**EXCEPTIONS**</u>

Disqualification under the sphere of Anti-Defection shall not apply in case where there is split or merger of $1/3^{rd}$ or more members of the party to another party. In simple words we can say that if $1/3^{rd}$ or more members of the party leaves and join another party, they will not be disqualified under the Anti-Defection law.However, this exception of $1/3^{rd}$ had been revised by the 91st Constitutional Amendment Act after which it now requires $2/3^{rd}$ members of the party members to merge with another members.

The major lacuna of the defection law is that hostility and enmity between the members of the party nurture internal disagreements with seniors, difference in opinion and beliefs and fight for governance, as a result of which members change and move from one party to another.

Defection machinery in India has a number of inadequacies and shortfalls, especially amid the recent instance of the Madhya Pradesh government crisis, in which JyotiradityaScindiawith 22 other MLAs left the party, which leadto the fall of Kamal Nath'sgovernment who is member of Indian Congress Party, and the Kerala legislative assembly case in 2019.

In order to foster Parliamentary Consensus, anti-defection rules were established in the Indian Constitution as a set of guidelines for elected officials to follow. When a person is nominated as a member of a political party and stands for office using that party's symbol, he owes loyalty tothe party and the citizens who contributed their precious votes. However, many leaders are leaving their parties to join the opposition, which can lead to the collapse of the government in that state, causing political unsteadiness. As a result, lawmakers must behave in accordance with the values of the party.

<u>SUGGESTIONS FOR REFORM</u>

LAW COMMISSION'S 170TH REPORT- Any provision which relievessplits and merger from disqualification to be deleted and political parties should limit issuing of whips to instances only when the government is in danger.

ELECTION COMMISSION- Decision given under the 10<u>th</u> schedule should be made by the President/Governor on the binding advice of the Election Commission.

CONSTITUTION REVIEW COMMISSION (2002)- The member so disqualified should be expelled from holding any public office or any remunerative political post for remaining time period. The votes casted by such members should be held invalid.[6]

<u>CONCLUSION</u>

Every law framed and implemented works magic when it sticks to the transparency and meticulousness. The rules and regulations framed under the Act should not only stabilize the governance but also help in reducing the political disparities and corruption in the nation, which will eventually lead to a developed nation. And this is possible when all the three wings of Indian Constitution work in harmony and at the same time keep check on each other. Under defection law it is more important for us to give the power of decision making in hands of judiciary instead of putting it in the legislative councils and assemblies, so that the ultimate resultis free from all the biasness and prejudice which might be present in the decision making of the speakers of such bodies. For that to happen reformation of the provisions are important to be ensured.

<u>Author's Bio</u>

Hello, my name is Neha Kachhawaha; I'm pursuing law as a Profession. I find that all the subjects in law are fascinating and practical at the same time, and after the completion of the degree, one can choose what field they need to go to as there are many career options.

MARITAL RAPE

Author: Yashika Mor, II year of B.A.,LL.B. from Geeta institute of law

Abstract

Marital rape has generated a great deal of discussion in India. In contrast to the majority of industrialised countries, India has not yet criminalised marital rape. Due to the patriarchal nature of Indian society, campaigners and the Indian media argue that marital rape should be made a crime there. However, a more conventional viewpoint contends that because Hinduism holds marriage in high regard, the institution shouldn't be endangered by criminalising marital rape.Despite being founded on the principle of justice, India has failed to recognise a woman's freedom to govern marital interactions as a component of equality. The only option left for victims of marital rape in the country is to file a lawsuit because there are no legal protections against it. Even though they have used a variety of methods to detect the crime and have imposed severe fines, courts are constrained and thus unable to define marital rape as "forceful intercourse by a man upon his wife" due to the absence of statutory criteria. The legislature is necessary because the judicial system is insufficient on its own.To reflect the situation of society today, the laws need to be revised. The government has presented two reasons before the Delhi High Court in support of its stance that marital rape shouldn't be made a criminal. First, criminalising marital rape would cause societal unrest because of India's stringent religious rules and the holy nature of marriage.Second, given the various unfounded charges that may be levelled against husbands, it shouldn't be considered a crime. Dismantling the presumptions held by the government and other Orthodox organisations is essential. Since what a woman perceives as rape may not be what other people would characterise as rape, the Indian government has claimed that marital rape cannot be criminalised.This claim shows how archaic Indian society is because it is now regularly used as a defence in rape cases. The victim and his or her permission are the only factors in a rape. If a woman feels violated, she will break the law. Only that standard shall be considered. The incident's or the woman's behaviour in this case's social perception cannot be a factor. Therefore, it doesn't matter whether the wife and others hold opposite opinions. This cannot be used as a defence to withhold justice from her or to deny that a rape occurred.

Introduction

Marital or spousal rape occurs when a spouse engages in sexual activity without consent. Lack of authorization is the crucial element, which need not involve physical violence. Marital rape is seen as a kind of domestic violence and sexual abuse. Having sex outside of marriage, which was once thought to be a right of couples, is now primarily considered as rape by many countries throughout the world, prohibited by international agreements, and increasingly criminalised.

Though that isn't always the case, women are more likely than males to endure marital rape. Marital rape is a common occurrence in abusive marriages and is a kind of ongoing victimisation. It is intricately intertwined with regional laws, social mores, and cultural norms that interact to shape each distinct event and circumstance in a distinctive way. Due to traditional views of marriage, interpretations of religious doctrines, ideas about male and female sexuality, and cultural expectations of a wife's subordination to her husband—views that are still prevalent in many parts of the world—non-consensual sex between married people is not criminalised or prosecuted.In the majority of Western countries, second-wave feminism in particular started to question these views on marriage and sexuality in the 1960s and 1970s. As a result, the woman's right to self-determination in all matters relating to her body was recognised and the exemption or defence of marital rape was eliminated.

In India, marital rape has a very long and difficult history. The legislation prohibiting marital rape had also been established and somewhat updated. Only a little bit had been changed. The issue of marital rape has not received as much attention as rape has. There is no legal definition of marital rape; rather, it is only described by some authors and political and legal theorists.A significant portion of the world has historically seen marital rape as a crime, tort, or theft of a man's property. Because property damage in the context of marital rape refers not to injury to the victim but rather to her father's or her husband's properties, some individuals believe that a husband cannot rape his wife. In light of this, it is obvious that a husband cannot be made to pay for raping his wife. A husband cannot rape his legally wedded wife if they are living together. Before the 20th century, it was thought that a woman's legal rights would be assumed by her legitimate husband once they were married.If you get married, your spouse won't be accountable for the rape you committed together, according to this theory. However, you would only be accountable for your own rape actions. According to several traditions, getting married does not require consent. Since consent is not required for sexual behaviour, it follows that it is not required for marriage. In some communities where the bride price is paid, even the wife's independence is compromised.While forced sex during marriage was authorised in some parts of Africa, women did have the right to reject in some situations, such as those following childbirth, throughout the menstrual cycle, or when a close relative passed away. Up until relatively recently, rape was viewed as a crime against honour and dignity under both domestic and international law. The Geneva Fourth Convention mandates that women be provided with further protection from offences against their honour, such as rape, forced prostitution, and other indecent attacks. Rape has only recently been recognised as a crime against women's autonomy, dignity, and reputation, having not been recognised as a violent crime against human dignity until 1990.She decided to put her dignity, reputation, freedom, and liberty before those of her father, family, or even her husband's honour. Some traditional myths hold that a female's virginity is the only property that is withheld from her, making her the father's property prior to marriage and the husband's property following it. A man cannot be held accountable for the rape because his wife was in her care at the time.Raping his second wife, however, might be viewed as a serious theft of that man's property (women's sexuality). The regulations that had been designed to safeguard the property interest that man had in his women—and not to defend themselves—were based on the belief that bride capture constituted stealing the father's property by raping his daughter. The idea that women are property has had an impact on marital rape ideologies and laws.

• <u>Is rape in a marriage a crime?</u>

Rape certainly violates a person's fundamental right to physical integrity and dignity, whether they are married or not. Because marital rape satisfies the requirements for an offence, including hurt, pain, a violation of a fundamental right, and the humiliation of women with the aim or mensrea, it may be possible to hold out hope that it may be prosecuted as a crime. These types of biases cause the law's application and enforcement to be inconsistent with its spirit. One might comprehend the purpose of the law given the current circumstances. In order to protect people from abuse and uphold the sacredness of the matrimonial institution, laws are developed.These are not utilised to defend the dignity of women or save the lives of battered women.

<u>Conclusion</u>

Marital rape in India has a very troubled and lengthy history. The law that forbids marital rape has also been developed and revised to some extent. There had been very little change. Compared to other rape-related issues, marital rape has not received as much attention. Marital rape is not legally defined; rather, it is only characterised by some writers and political and legal theorists. In many parts of the world, marital rape has been considered a crime, tort, or theft of a man's property.Marital rape is not a crime in India. In India, there is no absolute law governing that. Acts, regulations, and legislation pertaining to marital rape are either obscure or non-existent, and it also depends on how the courts interpret them. There is a rape provision in the IPC, but there is also an exception for marital rape: "Sexual intercourse of a man with his lawful wife, when the woman is not a minor, is not rape." According to Section 376 of the Criminal Code, which details the penalties for rape, a rapist may be detained for a period of time up to 10 years, rather than only 7 years. In addition, unless the woman was her own spouse, and at the penalty of penalties, she was not less than 12 years old.In this particular circumstance, the rapist may receive a minimum sentence of two years in jail. Both the penalty and the fine may be imposed. Therefore, it might be argued that if the spouse is under 15, the marital status will be taken into account. There is a misconception that a husband cannot rape his wife because possessions damage in a case of marital rape does not refer to harm to the victim but rather to her father or her husband's goods.Rape clearly breaches a person's fundamental right to physical integrity and dignity, regardless of whether they are married or not. Even though the Indian Constitution grants the rights to equality, liberty, and dignity to anybody who disagrees with the Indian people, this paradigm is rarely contested in practise.This notion holds that a marriage can be approved by the court. This clause is considered to mean that both parties to the marriage have given their consent. The phrase used completely diminishes women's rights. The Manusmriti is the sole basis for the notion that marriage shouldn't be messed with.Instead of overtly refusing sex in the Victorian era, it was said that doing so would lead a woman to violate her religious commitments and deviate from the path of the ideal wife. This particular argument fails to take into account the fact that marital rape is a particularly serious form of rape.

Author's Bio

My name is Yashika 2-year student of a law school. Born and brought up in Gohana (Sonipat) Since my school days, I had always been interested in law. When I did an extensive research about the details of the options, I realized that doing a BA LLB course would be more beneficial as the course covered company law and a law graduate can easily be appointed as a law officer of a company (if I wished to work in the corporate environment) . So, I chose the BALLB course. Currently I have just completed my 1st year at law and I am eagerly looking at all the aspects of this profession. I still have to decide as to what is going to be my specialization.

CHAPTER FOUR

GAMBIA VS. MYANMAR CASE

Author: Akriti Shukla, IV year of B.B.A.,LL.B. from Banasthali Vidhyapith

Gambia accuses Myanmar of historical genocidal acts 2019's The Gambia v. Myanmar case, which involves the genocide of the Rohingya, is being heard by the International Court of Justice

1. **Why has the genocide against the Rohingyas been covered in the media?**

Global media coverage of THE genocide of the Rohingya has been extensive. It has given international lawyers a chance to emphasize the importance of their profession.

This situation has undergone two significant developments. In 2019, an enquiry was opened at the International Criminal Court (the "ICC").

According to Article 7.1.d of the Rome Statute of the ICC, the Office of the ICC Prosecutor filed a request regarding the allegations of crimes against humanity involving the deportation or forceful transfer of population from Myanmar to Bangladesh.

Second, the Republic of the Gambia applied to the International Court of Justice (the "ICJ") alleging that the Republic of the Union of Myanmar violated the 1948 Convention on the Prevention and Punishment of the Crime of Genocide and requesting the ICJ to adopt preliminary measures.

2. What transpired in the ICJ case between The Gambia and Myanmar?

The International Court of Justice decided on January 23, 2020, after hearing from both sides, that Myanmar shall:

1. Follow the Convention's directives to "take all steps within its power to avoid the commission of all actions within the ambit of Article II;"

2. Confirm that its military did not engage in any of the behavior listed in (a), including complicity in genocide, direct and open incitement to commit genocide, and attempted genocide;

3. Take concrete steps to protect evidence pertaining to alleged activities covered by Article II of the Convention from being destroyed and to secure its preservation;

4. Report to the ICJ on all actions taken to carry out its order within four months of the order's date but thereafter every six months until the ICJ has reached a final determination.

The International Court of Justice's jurisdiction over the case was then contested by Myanmar on January 20, 2021. Four concerns were voiced by Myanmar.

First, the "Court lacks jurisdiction, or alternatively the application is inadmissible, since the genuine petitioner in these hearings is the Organization of Islamic Cooperation." The Gambia lacks standing under Article IX of the Convention to bring this issue before the ICJ, hence the application was inadmissible. As a result of Myanmar's reservation to Article VIII of the Convention, The Gambia was unable to legitimately take the ICJ, and as a result, the application was deemed to be inadmissible. The fourth defence claims that "the Court lacks jurisdiction, or alternatively, the application is inadmissible, as there was no dispute between The Gambia and Myanmar over the date of filing the Application commencing from the date of the Application being filed,"

On July 22, the ICJ issued a decision on their objections. The first, third, and fourth complaints were all dismissed by a unanimous vote. By a divided vote of 15 to 1, it also dismissed the second complaint. To ascertain whether The Gambia and Myanmar really had a dispute for the ICJ to decide, it is crucial to examine the judgment and the arguments put up by both parties.

3. The ICJ's determination that a dispute exists between The Gambia and Myanmar was made in what manner?

The Gambia's application is based on Article IX of the Convention, which says that:

"Disputes between both the Parties To the contract relating to the interpretation, application, or fulfillment of the present Convention, including those relating to a State's responsibility for a genocide or for any of the additional acts enumerated in article III, shall, at the request of any of the parties to the dispute, be submitted to the International Court of Justice." (I have underlined to emphasize)

Myanmar said that The Gambia was speaking on behalf of the International Organization of Islamic Cooperation (OIC). This was Myanmar's first disapproval.

According to Article IX of the Convention, Myanmar claimed that there was no disagreement between The Gambia and itself. It said that the accusations of genocide were political and not legal since they were represented in papers and remarks made by or at the OIC. Additionally, it claimed that there was no shared understanding of the competing viewpoints held by the parties who made up the dispute.

The Gambia refuted these assertions by citing remarks made by its President and Vice-President during the general discussion of the 74th session of the United Nations General Assembly (the "UNGA"), specifically that "Gambia is prepared to lead the combined effort for trying to take the Rohingya issue to the International Court of Justice."

The ICJ concluded that the mutual awareness defence is unpersuasive and supported The Gambia's allegations. It claimed that since Myanmar had not responded to the president and vice president of The Gambia's words, Myanmar had disproved their assertions. Basically, it was assumed that there was a conflict because of Myanmar's quiet.

The UN Fact-Finding Mission's 2018 report on Myanmar, remarks made by representatives of The Gambia and Myanmar before the UNGA, and a note-verbale delivered by The Gambia to Myanmar are all mentioned throughout the ruling.

Based on these three references, the International Court of Justice (ICJ) decided that The Gambia and Myanmar were involved in a dispute under Article IX of the Convention.

It is debatable whether the ICJ correctly read the references, especially in identifying a conflict under the first two references.

4. According to the parties' declarations, was there a conflict between Both the Gambia and Myanmar?

In other rulings, the ICJ has said that in order to establish the existence of a controversy, it is necessary to consider both bilateral and multilateral exchanges of remarks or documents between the parties. Specifically, "the creator document, real audience, and their substance," is given particular consideration by the ICJ while doing this, according to its statement. The remarks in issue in the current situation were made by the President and Vice-President of Gambia as well as the Union Minister for the Office of the State Counsellor of Myanmar.

While it is important to take these authorities' words into account when determining if there is a disagreement, it is their statements' substance that has to be emphasized. The Gambian President said that his nation would support an accountability system that would guarantee those responsible for the heinousgenocideagainst the Rohingya Muslims were brought to justice in this regard in 2019. The UN Fact-Finding Mission's conclusions were criticized three days later by Myanmar's Union Minister for the Office of the State Counsellor as being "based on narratives and not on real facts" in his statement to the UNGA.

The Gambia claims that these assertions make it very evident that the parties are at odds. But whether there was a disagreement between both the two parties as a result of these words alone is debatable.

The vice president of the Gambia further said that his country intended to "lead coordinated efforts to bring the Rohingya matter to the International Court of Justice." Two days later, the Union Minister of Myanmar's Office of the State Counselor rejected the UN Fact-Finding Mission's findings, calling it "biassed and defective, focused not on facts but on narratives."

These utterances, according to The Gambia, indicate that Myanmar was aware that The Gambia had opinions that differed from its own about Myanmar's legal obligations under the Convention.

While these remarks do suggest that The Gambia believed Myanmar had committed genocide, they do not suggest that there is any disagreement between the parties about the Convention. Myanmar has criticised the UN Fact-Finding Mission's findings in both remarks. Although it was not compelled to, it did not respond to The Gambia's assertion.

5. What effect did the findings of the UN Fact-Finding Mission have on the ICJ case?

The report of the UN Fact-Finding Mission has been frequently used by The Gambia and the ICJ. The remarks provided by Myanmar government representatives refute this story. This study provides the foundation for The Gambia's claim that Myanmar committed genocide.

According to the article, The Gambia's position appears to be that Myanmar has committed genocide. While The Gambia mentioned this study in its pronouncements, Myanmar casts doubt on it, suggesting that it does not agree that genocide was committed. This is considered to be a sign of a conflict between Myanmar and The Gambia.

This result seems to be a stretch of the case. Even if we were to believe it, it would not establish that Myanmar and The Gambia are involved in a conflict. The report's denial by Myanmar cannot be compared to The Gambia's denial of allegations.

However, the Gambia's allegations may be taken in one of two ways depending on Myanmar's quiet, therefore it is challenging to refute the ICJ's argument that there is a disagreement based on Myanmar's silence.

6. Does the Note Verbale that The Gambia addressed to Myanmar establish that the two parties are engaged in conflict?

A Note Verbale, sometimes known as a "verbal note," is a formal document communication between two nations. In this case, The Gambia addressed a Note Verbale to Myanmar after the UNGA comments, and it strongly cited the findings of the UN Fact-Finding Mission. Myanmar, however, didn't respond to the Note Verbale.

In light of the fact that Myanmar had previously rejected the report, shouldn't it have done so once again in its reply to The Gambia? What prevented it from repeating it in response to the Note Verbale? In any case, the claim that a disagreement existed should only have been based on Myanmar's failure to respond to the Note Verbale.

By a vote of 15 to 1, the International Court of Justice (ICJ) decided last month that "it has jurisdiction, on the basis of Article IX of the Convention on the Prevention and Punishment of the Crime of Genocide, to entertain the Application filed by the Republic of The Gambia on November 11, 2019, and that the said Application is admissible." Myanmar has until April 24,

2023, in which to file its countermemorial. The ICJ will then continue with the case's merits hearing.

As a result, The Gambia seems to have won the argument over whether there is a conflict between it and Myanmar.

CHAPTER FIVE

MEDICAL JURISPRUDENCE AND RELATED LAWS IN INDIA

Author: Abhinav Pandey, I year of B.A.,LL.B.(Hons.) from University of Lucknow

Introduction

Medical Jurisprudence is the application of medical knowledge in the legal field for providing justice in both criminal as well as civil cases.The Latin term 'Juris' stands for 'law' and 'Prudentia' stands for 'Knowledge'. Thereby, it is the domain which makes the use of the medically relevant facts and then integrates them with the legal system, providing assistance to the criminal justice system. In order to convict a probable offender, it is utmost important to know the relevancy of the evidences. Thus, the need of using scientific principles was felt. As this field grew, it gave immense power to the medical practitioner as they were now playing a very important role by having an expert opinion in the cases. But with this power came huge responsibilities. The doctor patient relation, medical negligence, ethical conducts, professional misconducts are a few to name. The field of medical jurisprudence is a very ancient field but with the advent of technology and the reforms being added in the legal system, this branch is always under development. In order to completely understand true meaning and its importance one should understand how actually did this field came into action.

History of Medical Jurisprudence

The History of medical jurisprudence dates back to 4000-3000 BC and the data recorded can be studied from the Materia Medica Imhotep around 2300 BC, the chief justice and the personal physician to the ruler of Egypt was considered as the first medico-legal expert.While in India, the Charaka Samhita around the 7th century BC contained rules related to the ethics, privilege, obligationsetc. mandatory to be followed by a Physician. Various other texts like Manusmriti, YajnavalkyaSmriti, Sushruta Samhitaetc. also played a majorrole in maintaining and regulating the medical practice.An autopsy is considered as the most important tool in medicolegal practice. In the 18th century Dr. Edward Bulkley was the first to do a medico-legal autopsy in India.With the introduction of this branch in India, it didn't take much of a time for it to grow in all directions. In 1822, the state of Calcutta got the countries first Medical School. This development further proceeded to the states of Bombay and Madras .Over the last few decades, the scientific techniques have advanced by multiple folds. The tests performed and the results obtained are so precise that they can act as evidence, sufficient in itself to prove or disprove a convict. This growth has also led to the enlargement and thus diversification of medical jurisprudence into numerous small branches.To fit more accurately in the present time, the term medical jurisprudence has mostly been replaced by the new terminology 'forensic science'.

Some of the major branches in Forensic Medicine are

1.Forensic Odontology

Forensic odontology is a branch of forensic medicine and, in the interests of justice, deals with the proper examination, handling, and presentation of dental evidence in a court of law.The work of a forensic odontologist covers the following:

1.Analysis of weapon marks using the principles of bite-mark Analysis

2.Presentation of bite and weapon mark evidence in court as an expert witness

3.Assistance in building up a picture of lifestyle and diet at an Archeological Sites.

2.ForensicPathology

Forensic pathology is a field of forensic science which involves application of pathological methods in investigation of a crime and of sudden, suspicious or unexplained deaths. A forensic pathologist examines bodies in order to determine the cause of death and circumstances surrounding the cause of death as well as looks for evidence that can be used in trials.

3.Forensic Anthropology

Forensic Anthropology is a special sub field of Physical Anthropology the study of human remains that involves applying skeleton analysis and techniques in archaeology to solving criminal cases. When human remains or a suspected burial are found forensic Anthropologists are called upon to gather information from the bones and their recovery context to determine who died, how long ago they died and how they died. Forensic Anthropologists specialize in Analyzing hard tissues such as bones.

4.Forensic Toxicology

Forensic toxicology is the application of toxicology to the field of law. The discipline continues to flourish as a result of human fascination with poisons, their effects on living organisms, detection in human remains, and role of toxicology in judicial proceedings, forensic drug testing, and human performance toxicology are the three major subdivisions of the discipline at the present time. Forensic toxicology investigations begin with the fundamental and critical requirement of acquisition of an appropriate specimen.

<u>**The Major Professions involved in Legal Cases are**</u>

Medicine Department- consisting of Doctors, Pharmacists Nurses,

Legal Department-consisting of Judges, lawyers, Police

For enhancing the knowledge of a personnel of medical background different courses in forensic medicine have been introduced in their curriculum. Along with providing legalguidance this course focuses on training the doctors in the major advancements in the forensic medicine field, their responsibilities, ethics, rights, etc.By providing scientific evidence and assisting the judiciary and legal system, the medical field helps in strengthening the ultimate of providing justice and thereby, benefitting all.The legal practitioners i.e., the lawyers who may have to time and again encounter the medical issues in their practice are hardly aware about the medical language, knowledge, profession and the associated complexities of this profession.The Medical Practitioners are also humans and it is impossible for them to be unerring. When a simple mistake of a doctor leads to the loss of a life, he is answerable to the system.In a hypothetical case, if a patient dies due to a hypersensitive allergic reaction from a certain drug, which is widely accepted by the majority of the population then is the death to be considered as the fault of the doctor. The patient's family may file a report against the doctor for medical negligence. The lawyers working on the case on behalf of the doctor and the patient, should have ample knowledge for understanding the reasons which led to the sudden death. This is how medical jurisprudence will help in determining whether the doctor is supposed to be held guilty or not. Many times, in a bizarre circumstance, the doctors keep aside their legal restrictions and prioritize the patient's wellbeing and this often leads them as guilty in the court. To avoid and keep such actions under a check, hospitals have their own legal firms who timely monitor the work of the doctors.While considering medical jurisprudence one cannot brush aside certain controversial areas like role of doctor for evidence collection from crime scene, mercy killing, organ transplantation, medical negligence, civil negligence, therapeutic misadventure, etc.

From the world of fiction to reality, the cases of Anaesthetic and Operative Deaths are always under the limelight.

The causes of death due to anaesthetic agents can be found out via post-mortem examination. These causes may include; hypersensitivity, cardiac arrest, respiratory inadequacy, etc. The cardiac arrest and respiratory failure are the most common modes of death.These cases often invite an investigation on the medical personals involved in the procedure. Legal department overlaps here with the medical department and helps in figuring out whether it was a medical negligence or a medical Maloccurence. Some of the most common cases under medical jurisprudence include:

1.Injury and Wounds

Wounds, a break in the continuity of any bodily tissue due to violence, where violence is understood to encompass any action of external agency, including, for example, surgery.

2.Paternity Testing

DNA paternity testing is an important tool used to prove or disprove a biological parent-child relationship. The test uses a DNA (deoxyribonucleic acid) profile for each individual and compares the data to determine if there is a genetic match. If the child and potential non-gestational parent genetically match, then they are the biological parent. If the data does not match, then they are excluded as the biological parent.

3.Cause and Manner of Death

The cause of death can be either natural or unnatural. For example, if a head injury is the cause of death broadly, then how the head injury occurred can be accidental, suicidal, or homicidal

4.Death due to Poisons

Any substance that can cause severe organ damage or death if ingested, breathed in, injected into the body or absorbed through the skin. Many substances that normally cause no problems, including water and most vitamins, can be poisonous if taken in excessive quantity. Poison treatment depends on the 'substance.

LAWS RELATED TO MEDICAL JURISPRUDENCE IN INDIA

(INDIAN PENAL CODE, 1860)

Section 44 of IPC

The Provision provides the definition of Injury as any harm whatever illegally caused to any person in body, mind, reputation, or property.

Section 319 IPC

The provision lays down the definition of hurt as bodily pain, disease, or infirmity caused to any person.

Section 320 IPC

This provision defines grievous injury and lays down a list of injuries that comes under the broad head of grievous injury. Any of the following injuries is grievous:

1.Emasculation

2.Permanent privation of sight of either Eye

3.Permanent privation of the hearing of either ear

4.Destruction or permanent impairing of powers of any member or joint

5.Fracture or dislocation of tooth or bone

Any hurt which Endangers life, or which causes the Victim to be in severe bodily pain, or unable to follow his ordinary pursuits for a period of Twenty day.

Section 321 IPC

The section defines "Voluntarily Causing Hurt".

Section 322 IPC

The section defines "Voluntarily Causing Grievous Hurt".

Section 351 IPC

Defines Assault Attempt to apply force. Whoever makes any gesture or preparation intending or knowing it to be likely that such gesture or preparation will cause any person present to apprehend that he who makes the gesture or preparation is about to use criminal force to that person, is said to commit an assault.

Section 323 IPC

The section defines Punishment for Voluntarily Causing Hurt. Shall be imprisonment which may extend for One year with or without fine which may be One Thousand Rupees.

Section 324 IPC

The Section defines Punishment for Voluntarily Causing Hurt by dangerous weapon shall be imprisonment for up to Three years with or without fine.

Section 325 IPC

The section defines Punishment for Voluntarily Causing Grievous Hurt. Shall be imprisonment which may extend for Seven years with or without fine.

Section 326 IPC

The section describes Punishment for Voluntarily Causing Grievous Hurt by dangerous weapon or means. Shall be imprisonment for life or for Ten years with or without fine.

Section 328 IPC

The section describes Punishment of causing hurt using poison, etc., shall be imprisonment up to Ten years with or without fine.

(INDIAN EVIDENCE ACT, 1872)

Section 45

The provision deals with the Opinions of experts. When the Court has to form an opinion upon a point of foreign law or of science or art, or as to identity of handwriting, the opinions upon that point of persons especially skilled in such foreign art, law or science , are relevant facts. Such persons are called experts.

Section 114A

In a prosecution for rape, where the question is whether sexual intercourse was without the consent of the woman, and she states in her evidence that she did not consent, the court shall presume that she did not consent.

(CODE FOR CRIMINAL PROCEDURE, 1973)

Section 53 (i) CrPC

An accused may be examined by a Medical Practitioner/Doctor at the request of a Police officer using reasonably necessary force.

Section 53 (ii) CrPC

Whenever the person of a female accused is to be examined, the examination shall be made only by or under the supervision of a female registered medical practitioner.

Section 54 CrPC

An arrested person may be examined at his request by a medical practitioner to detect evidence in his favour.

Section 174 CrPC

Police to enquire and report on suicide, etc.

Section 176 CrPC

Inquiry by Magistrate into cause of death.

(INDIAN MEDICAL COUNCIL ACT,1956)

Section 20A- Professional conduct

The Council may prescribe standards of professional conduct and etiquette and a code of ethics for Doctors.

Regulations made by the Council under sub-sectionmay specify which violations thereof shall constitute infamous conduct in any professional respect, that is to say, professional misconduct, and such provision shall have effect notwithstanding anything contained in any law for the time being in force.According to the Current Indian Scenario, there are certain drawbacks with respect to these laws.Irrespective of having several indispensable benefits, the evidences procured via medical jurisprudence are still considered under the expert opinion rather than a Primary evidence.Under theIndian Evidence Act, 1872only in certain cases the report of an autopsy procedure is considered as a documentary evidence.Doctors are bounded by the Doctor-Patient confidentiality and this often places them in a dilemma of whether to share the information or not with the legal system.If it is in the doctor's knowledge that any of hispatient has committed a crime other than suicide, then he is bound to inform the Legal Authorities. In failing to do so, he may be punished.Thus, clear briefing to the doctors on these Pre-Existing Laws and Amendment in certain conflicting laws is the need of the hour.

A few suggestions would be legal drafting of legislation which will consider the evidences of medical jurisprudence as a primary evidence.

Other scientific test results, when performed under standard testing protocol, must also be considered as documentary evidences.

If a patient tries to commit suicide the doctor must report to the concerned authorities as this may help in resolving the factors which may have led to such a huge step by the victim and also ensure the patients safety in the near future.

Medical jurisprudence plays a very crucial role in bridging this gap between the doctors and the lawyers. This field has contributed to the society by opening the new doors to those old pending cases, which were once considered to be stuck at a dead end.

Jurisprudence of emergency medical care in India

In India in the 1980, Emergency Medical care Jurisprudence, which closely intersected ethical concerns, established the groundwork for the emergence of healthcare litigations. In following litigations involving the medical profession and private and public healthcare providers, it provided a bridge for the courts to apply the right to a dignified life and the State's constitutional responsibility to save a life. It also made it easier to write healthcare jurisprudence and declare healthcare to be a Fundamental Right.

The topic of emergency medical treatment, which frequently involves dealing with life and death circumstances, brings various overlapping concerns about health services, patient rights, and the state's and medical profession's responsibilities into sharp light. The indignity caused by the refusal to treat critically ill patients, resulting in death, undue suffering, morbidity, and financial loss, has been challenged in courts on the basis of moral-ethical principles that are at the heart of the medical profession and the reason behind the healthcare system in a welfare state.

By standers do not come forward to aid the victims of such emergency situations because of the medico-legal nature of the cases and the fear of being harassed by the police and courts. Following a PIL filed by the save live Foundation in 2012, the Honourable Supreme Court of India made efforts in 2016 to enact new legislation relating to accidents and emergency treatment by requesting that the Central Government draft guidelines for the protection of 'Good Samaritans' from police or other authorities. Santosh Ahlawat, an MP, raised the issue in Parliament. In another key ruling Pt. Parmand and KataraVs. Union of Indiaand Ors (1989), the subject of safeguarding doctors from legal headaches in medico-legal matters so that they can offer prompt treatment to patients in need of emergency life-saving care has been addressed.

In the well-known case of Paschim Banga Khet Mazdoor Samiti Vs. State of West Bengal (1996), the victim, Hakim Sheikh, was an agricultural labourer who was a member of the Paschim Banga Khet Mazdoor Samiti, a labour organisation. He was denied admission to five public hospitals after falling off a moving train on his way to work. The patient was refused admission on the ground that there were no beds available. The victim was finally admitted to a private hospital and forced to pay expensive fees for his care. Surprisingly, some Twenty years after the Paschim Banga Khet Mazdoor Samiti case, the focus in "the Good Samaritan" discourse has changed from the healthcare system to the healthcare of individuals from a different social class. This discourse has been pushed into the public imagination without any mention of emergency care accessibility and availability for the disadvantaged. It appears sufficient that such care is available, through medical insurance, to the upper-middle class, who continue to overlook its inaccessibility to the underprivileged.

Role of Public Interest Litigation in developing Medical Jurisprudence

A number of subsequent PIL aided in the development of personhood jurisprudence, affirming the priority of the right to life and dignity. As a result, Article 21 of the Indian Constitution became the bedrock of social and civil-political rights, including health and healthcare. The right to medical treatment for employees and civil rights litigation for the rights of people in jails and police custody are two of the many components of a large number of healthcare litigations. Even though the number of lawsuits involving emergency medical treatment is less, they have shown systemic flaws in the field of life-saving care. These include medical practitioners' insensitivity and personal/professional apathy, especially towards patients from socially disadvantaged groups, as well as delays or denials of care.

Medical care in Police Custody or Judicial Custody

People in state custody, such as those in police or judicial custody, as well as those in state-run asylums and prisons, are subjected to torture, ill-treatment, and abuse, as well as are denied access to necessary medical care. In Poonam Sharma v. Union of India, the Delhi High Court reaffirmed police officers' and physicians' constitutional obligations to care for wounded people in medico-legal matters. Article 32 of the Constitution, which establishes access to justice as a fundamental right, confirms the indisputable nature of the State commitment.

Viewing patients availing healthcare services as consumers

The ramifications of violating the principles of saving lives and the duty of care are clearly stated in the medical jurisprudence. Failure to give prompt medical treatment to a person in need of emergency care is claimed to be a breach of Article 21 of the Indian Constitution, which guarantees the right to life. As a result of this rationale, the medical profession was brought within the Consumer Protection Act of 1986. The medical profession, as represented by medical groups, has fought for more than a decade to put healthcare workers in general, and physicians in particular, under the Consumer Protection ion Act1986.

The case of Indian Medical Association Vs. V.P. Shantha (1995) exemplifies the medical profession's long-standing opposition to any regulation of doctors under the guise of professional self-regulation. In this case, the definition of 'service' as it relates to healthcare under various circumstances was argued in order to ascertain the consumer status of the healthcare-seeking patient. The lawsuits pointed out the rejection of admission to public hospitals, which almost always results in death or treatment in private hospitals. Medical malpractice and ethical problems at private hospitals were also mentioned which include the termination of medical care due to a lack of immediate payment, medical malpractice, and the charging of unreasonable fees for treatment.

Conclusion

Both the Legal fields and Medical fields have Profited greatly from the development of medical Jurisprudence. A greater understanding and cooperation have evolved, allowing both disciplines to operate more smoothly. With the advancement of Medical Jurisprudence, formerly insoluble problems are now easily settled. It may be used to identify a child paternity as well as the Identification of Human remains that have been disfigured beyond recognition in Incidents such as factory explosions, and so on. It may be used to solve instances involving rape, murder in the subject of Evidence laws. After a Person has died, Medical Jurisprudence procedures like an Autopsy can be used to uncover key information that is Crucial to the case. The Heart of ethics, Codified in the Code of Medical Ethics and strengthened by ethical jurisprudence, may revitalise ethics compliant healthcare in India. Streamlining ethics in the private and public healthcare systems would necessitate a number of policy measures, including a complete statute to institutionalise ethical principles for maintaining the right to healthcare.

<u>Author's Bio</u>

Abhinav Pandey is someone who is constantly Excited and ready for the next chapter of his Life. He is contemporary But compassionate Writer who tries to infuse his work with a wide range of experience, And ideas. He enjoys Being able to make His writing relatable to others by generalizing The ideas he is writing About.

CHAPTER SIX

AAZADI KA AMRIT MAHOTSAV

Author: Anchal Verma, I year of B.A.,LL.B. from University of Lucknow, Faculty of Law

We, as an Indian feel overwhelmed with extreme joy and excitement on hearing the word 'azadi'. A word which was once merely a dream to achieve is now at the doorstep of its Diamond anniversary. It marks a moment to cherish and admire our achievements and glories as we celebrate the 'Azadi Ka Amrit Mahotsav' on 15th August, 2022. In fact, it is an attempt by Government of India to celebrate, cherish and honour 75th years of independence and the magnificent last of its citizens, culture and achievements. Commencing 75 weeks ahead of its 75th year of independence, this mahotsava will last till 15th August, 2023.

It aims at encouraging the youth of the nation to come up with their ideas and to pave the way forward for the Independent India; a nation independent in its actions, policies and most significantly, a nation which considers people as its sovereign. The Mahotsav launched with an objective of creating a vision for the country in 2047 sustains on the basis of its pillars of struggle for independence, ideas and achievements, actions and resolutions of 75 years. These pillars are meant to make the younger generation aware of the history and struggle for independence. As our honourable Prime Minister, Shri Narendra Damodardas Modi, has aptly said, " The Azadi Amrit Mahotsav means elixir of energy of independence; elixir of inspirations of the warriors of freedom struggle; elixir of new ideas and pledges; and elixir of Aatmanirbharta. Therefore, this Mahotsav is a festival of awakening of the nation; festival of fulfilling the dream of good governance; and the festival of global peace and development." Indeed, it is a tribute to the warriors of the freedom struggles, to those who renered their services for the development of the nation and are still working for the upliftment of its citizens.

Indians are fortunate enough to witnesses the completion of 75 years of their Independence but certain questions still remain unanswered; Are we really entering in the amrit kaal ? The question of poors dying of starvation, the suffering of people in annually flooded areas, the deteriorating condition of press freedom raises a question before every Indian to ponder over the celebration of this Amrit Mahotsava. Will this celebration be worth remembering if one segment of the country feels alienated or goes to bed with an empty stomach. In the 2021, in Global Hunger Index, India ranked 101st out of the 116 countries with a score of 27.5, indicating the level of hunger that is serious. The wave of Covid-19 has forced many to shift to the below poverty line section. This occurred despite government's attempt to provide every poor household with the free ration throughout the pandemic. The situation would have been even more horrific in absence of such initiatives.

The situation seems to be more tense on observing the report 'Democracy under Seige' by the Freedom House. As per this report, India's status as a free country has changed to "partly free". It states that that there has been growing political influence on the social activists and press media. The incidents of CAA protest and migration due to sudden lockdown was violative of citizen's right. Moreover, government's ignorant response towards such issues not only questions the policies of the government but also makes us contemplate the extent of democratically elected government's accountability.

'Har Ghar Tiranga' is an another campaign under the celebration of Azadi Ka Amrit Mahotsav to encourage people to bring the Tiranga home and to hoist it to mark the 75th year of India's independence. No doubt, our national flag means a lot to every Indian Citizen. Pinning a Tiranga at homes, is indeed a symbolic representation of our personal connection, sentiments and commitment towards the task of nation building. It may even denote the idea of 'Unity in Diversity' that besides being from different religion, caste, class and states we as a citizen stand united for the national cause. We may have different views, ideologies and attitudes towards an issue but when it comes to the interest of nation, we stand united as an Indian besides our varied identities. But unfortunately, the reality stands far away from these illusions. Can merely pinning our national flag at our homes be the guarantor of our patriotism. If this applies, many deserving people would be devoid of the title of being patriotic. Where and how a daily wage earner will pin the flag who spends his nights on footpath, who finds it difficult to meet his both ends and for whom to have a cloth on his body is a blessing.

Also, on this special occasion of Azadi Ka Amrit Mahotsav, it would be injustice if one the strongest pillar of the society – women, remain untouched. They have built up a world for themselves. None of the field remained untouched by them. However, there body also remains easily accessible to all. Even today the cases of rapes and violence against women have surged up. This makes us ponder over the way forward for them.

Observing this Mahotsava merely as celebration and remembrance of the valour and valiance is not enough. Responsibility accompanies the Maturity. Since India will complete its 75 years of Independence on 15th August, 2022, it reaches its maturity age. It becomes its responsibility to maintain the democratic structure within and outside country on international forum and increase the extent of its accountability. The river of amrit is worth praising if it remains accessible to all. No one should be deprived of it. Also, we can can not conclude something as amrit by the time natural death becomes the only reason of human's death. Therefore, attempts should be made so that Amrit Kaal does not witnesses starvation. The communal hatred needed to be clamped upon else it may ruin the country from within.

Hope that equally accessible Amrit Dhara will flow throughout the country and all citizens will take a deep bath in it and feel relaxed. Let's hope for the positive.... What ends as achievement commences from a mere hope...!

• 37 •

CHAPTER SEVEN

THE LEGAL NET OF METAVERSE

Author: Duvvuru Sravya Reddy, III year of B.B.A.,LL.B. from IFIM Law School

<u>Abstract</u>

As we see it, the future of the internet is here. Remember when making video chats on a handheld device felt like science fiction a decade ago? Well, everything just became much more actual. Nowadays, we use virtual spaces for business meetings and family get-togethers. Virtual world become a part and parcel in life , especially after the COVID - 19 pandemic. People became more used to get things in hand without even moving leg for single inch using the modern technology.

<u>WHAT IS METAVERSE?</u>

Metaverse is a 3D technology, which is a combination of different virtual worlds. It can simply be understood as future version of internet. Metaverse is a quick developing idea. This concept of metaverse is still under construction. Speaking of Metaverse now, is just like speaking of internet in 1960s. Metaverse is a evolving virtual social platform.

Humanity has already made a start in this direction in the real world during the COVID-19 epidemic, with schooling moving online and virtual meetings replacing corporate travel on a scale that has never been thought possible. A lot of individuals also think that the metaverse's growth represents the Internet's natural transition from Web 2.0 to Web 3.0. For background, Web 1.0 is sometimes referred to as the beginning of Internet evolution, during which time users mostly consumed content. Users can also use the Internet to produce and exchange content when using Web 2.0, the prevalent paradigm at the moment. With the addition of disintermediation (the eventual elimination of middlemen) and decentralization in Web 3.0, people now have a great deal of autonomy over how they use the Internet.

The term "metaverse" broadly, refers to the movement of numerous aspects of the human experience, from the real world to an immersing virtual environment. The metaverse is fundamentally a clear junction of technology and content. Video games like Roblox and Fortnite, for instance, let players enter a large, sophisticated virtual environment and partake in a wide range of virtual experiences and exchanges, including those with other players from all over the world. Through platforms like Sensorium, users may establish their own alter egos and enter a shared virtual environment, where top DJs perform in front of a sizable audience of other users. In a recent announcement, Facebook introduced Horizon World, a "mixed reality" meeting environment that enables users to take part in meetings in a virtual setting complete with avatars, virtual meeting spaces and tables, and even virtual chalkboards. Utilizing digital characters and other artefacts, players can explore the real environment on some platforms, such as Pokémon Go and Illust Space.There isn't currently a single metaverse experience, despite references to "The Metaverse." Instead, "The Metaverse" refers to a concept that is most likely to be implemented in a number of virtual worlds, where technology has the potential to introduce material to those worlds in previously unimaginable ways, along with problems and legal issues that have never been thought of.

Advantages of Metaverse

1. Minimizes physical distance and connects the world

In some ways, the metaverse will serve as a neutral setting where people can interact as equals. Additionally, it will be simpler and more real to meet individuals who share your interests and viewpoints, allowing you to feel more at ease making new acquaintances while remaining in the comfort of your own home.

2. Improved social interactions through online

Internet wasn't the most interactive experience, but it was the only chance to communicate with other people during the Covid quarantine.In contrast, social interactions and events in the metaverse are far more immersive, enabling users to feel a close connection to their friends and loved ones. In the metaverse, gatherings, events, and performances can all be planned. Any function or family gathering you might wish to attend no longer depends on physical proximity.

3. Modernized social media

The most common phrase in usage over the last ten years is definitely "social media." Twitter and other platforms like Facebook (Meta) rely on the social component of the internet. And there is no doubt that the transition to a three-dimensional virtual environment will be advantageous for them. A very potent combination will allow us to experience social media like never before by fusing the capacity to construct virtual spaces in the metaverse with the potential of social media to create shared online worlds.

4. New marketing strategies

The metaverse will probably offer even more opportunities, similar to how social media has assisted in the creation of several business opportunities and gave rise to a new type of marketing and advertising on its platforms.

With the help of innovative marketing and advertising techniques like virtualized storefronts, curated shows, highly interactive participation, and customer service, the metaverse offers a wholly immersive way to advertise and consume goods and services. This is an alternative to just looking at everything on your phone's little screen. As a result, you may use haptic technology to see, grasp, and even feel the object (experience of touch through vibration, forces, and motion). Both the customer and the business will gain from this form of contact because both sides will have a better user experience.

5. Online education

Learning will be easier than ever thanks to the metaverse. It is no longer necessary to consider the classroom's actual location. In a practical learning setting, people from all over the world will be able to exchange knowledge and study alongside one another in real-time.

Additionally, since we have complete control over what the students see inside the metaverse, visual learning will make it simpler to communicate ideas and concepts. Since historical events would be experienced by the students directly rather than only conceptually, to truly experience life then, picture yourself exploring the streets of ancient Rome.

6. Gaming improvements

The first industry to gain from VR and AR technologies was gaming. In 2021, we saw the emergence of numerous brand-new VR games, and as technology develops, the games get better. This reality is being recognized by many game development studios, and they are starting to integrate their games into the metaverse. Leaders in this industry include Epic, which will invest $1 billion in gaming in the metaverse in early 2021.

Additionally, Meta (previously known as Facebook) renamed the entire business as the pioneer of the metaverse. This is in addition to other well-known businesses like Roblox and Microsoft with their Xbox metaverse.

7. Work environment improvements

The infinite office is a brand-new workspace idea that Mark Zuckerberg mentioned when he unveiled the metaverse. It promises to make working from home the best experience possible by enhancing convenience and boosting general productivity.

New technologies have always been utilised in the workplace. And nothing will change once the metaverse and VR technology are fully developed. It's an intriguing idea that will probably help many people to put on VR glasses and participate in a three-dimensional virtual replica of your workplace from the comfort of your home.

<u>Disadvantages of Metaverse</u>

1. Cybercrimes

Cybercrime is a significant issue that has existed on the internet since its inception. Governments have fought against it for years and invested millions of dollars, which has improved the security of our contemporary internet infrastructure. However, because the metaverse is a relatively new idea, it still lacks these high standards for cyber security. Due to this, it is very susceptible to all kinds of criminal activity, including, but not limited to, fraud, money laundering, child exploitation, trafficking in illicit products and services, and cyberattacks. Governments' limited ability to resist and combat cybercrime is another cause for concern because of the decentralized nature of the metaverse.

2. Negative impact on Cultures

One drawback of bringing everyone so close together and combining all the world's civilizations into one is losing the stunning cultural diversity that exists today. People won't feel linked to their own immediate civilization or the urge to embrace their own local or regional culture if they spend the most of their time in the metaverse. As a result, many long-standing customs that have been part of society since the dawn of time may finally come to an end, and a new civilization, while unifying and all-encompassing, may prove to be boring and uninteresting.

3. Privacy and security issues

People are often unaware that their data is being gathered and sold to advertising, among other things, which has always raised privacy concerns on the internet. The fact that Meta is paving the way for the new metaverse only makes these worries worse. Given their prior experiences with user privacy issues, this is a problem that hasn't gone away just because they changed their name.

4. Addictive

Gaming addiction can develop into a problem. Some claim that because you are totally submerged in a virtual world, there is a higher risk of addiction with the metaverse. Apart from meeting your basic bodily needs like eating and sleeping, you can stay in your VR setup.

Children and teenagers are especially at risk because, according to experts, allowing people under the age of 18 to spend too much time in the metaverse will seriously impair their development.

Furthermore, it could be challenging to distinguish between the real world and the virtual world if one lives in a virtual state. It will be difficult to strike a compromise between limiting adults' and teenagers' access to the metaverse while attempting to prevent addictive behavior.

5. Corporate takeover

When social media first emerged, it was intended to allow users like you and me to create content and engage with that of others. before large businesses seized control. The best example of this is probably when businesses entered the YouTube market and took control away from individual creators. As a result, we saw a shift from amateur, authentic videos to professionally produced and edited videos created by teams of experts.

6. Virtual bullying

The internet has a reputation for being a terrible place where strangers are frequently unkind and intolerant of others' differences. All across the internet, whether it is in social media or games, people engage in malicious behaviour toward others. Despite many initiatives to stop or restrict those actions. These negative actors will gain more control if consumers can experience the metaverse in full 3D on the internet. Because there is no longer a screen to look away from, there are more opportunities for people to attack others, which could leave victims less protected and more exposed.

7. Paves way for decreases physical interactions

How simple it is to lose track of time when you're in the metaverse is one of the main worries that a lot of people have about it. Your senses are essentially impaired, or to put it another way, they are linked to the digital world rather than the physical one. If exposed to the metaverse for an extended period of time, some individuals may lose their sense of connection to reality and even go so far as to deny the existence of any world other than the virtual one.

With the advent of mobile devices, where the average American spends around 5.4 hours per day staring at a screen, we do experience this type of behaviour to some extent today.

The legal net of Metaverse

Data privacy laws in India

Under the Information Technology Act of 2000, a series of regulations known as the Information Technology Rules, 2011, oversee the current data protection system. These regulations state that a business must have information security policies that encompass technological, operational, and physical security measures as well as written security plans to demonstrate code compliance.

In a notification dated February 25, 2021, the government published the Information Technology (Intermediary Guidelines and Digital Media Ethics Code) Rules, 2021 (IT Rules), with the main objective of regulating and safeguarding consumers from various potentially hazardous contents. The company must adhere to exact technological and design requirements in order to meet the standards for data accuracy, choice, consent, disclosure, portability, and security. The firm must also set up management processes to enforce outdated rules, privacy standards, and suggestions that are appropriate for the volume of information needed.

There are five legal and regulatory concerns

- Privacy & Security Issues
- Antitrust and competition laws are applied
- IPR Violations
- Possession of Responsibility
- Concerns Regarding Jurisdiction

Anti-trust and Competition laws application

The applicability of current laws has been contentious because of the peculiar nature of the metaverse. Since the beginning of the metaverse, anti-trust has been wrestling with existential questions.

A contract, combination, or conspiracy to obstruct trade, as well as monopolization, attempted monopolization, or conspiracy or combination to monopolize, are all prohibited under the Competition Act of 2002, which enforces antitrust laws. Unreasonable constraints are also forbidden. As a result, this legislation can be used if several apps compete in a market, and one unfairly dominates or poses a threat of doing so.

While the majority of anti-competitive behaviours, that exist in the real world can also exist in some form in the metaverse, the fundamental characteristics of the metaverse and the blockchain make it impossible to identify and crack down on such behaviour, allowing businesses to engage in it with impunity.

Private blockchains can be used by anti-competitive businesses, to exchange commercially sensitive information, like information about prices, among themselves. Only those who have the owner of the blockchain's permission, can access these blockchains. Authorities won't be able to access these messages and, as a result, prosecute such behaviour; however, they may demand such information, in accordance with the applicable laws. In contrast to the existing situation, where authorities can simply inspect enterprises' facilities, to acquire information about such violations.

Intellectual property rights Infringement

Since the creation of the Metaverse, the market for virtual accessories has grown; as people's commitment to their avatars grows, they are more likely to spend real money on virtual fashion accessories for them. Due to how simple it is to copy virtual goods, Metaverse has seen an increase in charges of trademark infringement. Businesses are now worried about their trademarks being used online in addition to on physical products.

While there is now a gap in government regulation that can offer remedies for virtual IPR-infringements, blockchain technology may offer businesses a workaround. Since a blockchain is an everlasting and unchangeable record of data, information entered into it cannot be removed or altered unless a consensus process is applied.

When a company's virtual products or services are available on more than one Metaverse platform, this technology can be deployed. The intellectual property rights in content connected to products and services are incorporated and protected by this technology. Attached are descriptions of the pertinent goods, ownership information, and the range of the pertinent rights. The applications that are legal and illegal for the product can be determined using this information. Furthermore, even if the product switches between platforms, this data remains connected to it during its entire digital life. This allegedly works well to safeguard a brand's intellectual property.

Obligation to Enforcement

Because no single user may alter the data on a blockchain without the consent of other users, as was already mentioned, blockchain technology significantly increases security. Pseudonymity, or the inability to determine a user's real identify even if their virtual identity is known, is another crucial feature of blockchain technology.

Despite these potential benefits, there are also very particular and distinct issues with blockchain technology. For instance, if one virtual character bothers another. Will the harasser be held accountable for their behaviour? Due to the lack of knowledge and application of law in such worlds, law enforcement would be challenging because authorities would be unable to hold anyone accountable for their actions in the metaverse.

Privacy & Security Issues

The Metaverse platform is likely to collect enormous amounts of sensitive personal data given the anticipated number of users. Any AR-VR device's privacy statement will often state that it will collect data on a user's biological characteristics, physical environment, and other private information. Due to the collection of such biometric data, this would be considered "sensitive personal data" under the IT Rules.

The government may issue orders allowing the interception and decryption of data in order to "protect the security, sovereignty, or integrity of the state," as stated in Section 69 of the IT Act. Data in the Metaverse environment can be monitored by the government, and if it is deemed to be against public policy, it can be withheld. The company can also be fined for breaking the rules. Though it remains to be seen how successful this is in practice, it is predicted that the law will inject itself in the metaverse period in a way that strikes a balance between essential rights, including freedom of expression, and the protection of the public interest.

<u>Concerns Regarding Jurisdiction</u>

Given that users of Metaverse are likely to come from a variety of backgrounds, countries, and regions, it is important to consider which country's laws would govern the virtual world and Metaverse ecosystem. In a borderless virtual environment, jurisdiction will be even more ambiguous, which is a major source of worry for many government organizations.

There is still a lot of confusion around the authorities' position on this matter, and none has been provided. The only workable solution is to collaborate and create laws jointly. The regulations must change in reaction to shifting dynamics, adding a variety of measures to address fresh problems and offer the world remedies.

<u>Conclusion</u>

A virtual environment called the metaverse has its own rules. Jurisdiction is my favourite legal issue to discuss in the Metaverse. Think of the opportunities! I'll be bringing the popcorn so I can watch these discussions from the front row.

Real-world laws and substantive laws are similar, but not the same. Knowing which laws apply to Metaverse is crucial if you intend to engage in behaviour that is prohibited in the real world. These are only a few of the most prevalent categories of legislation that are applicable in the Metaverse.

In conclusion, the danger for Metaverse users is increased because there are currently no explicit regulations in India that control Metaverse in a reasonable manner. There is a legal gaping hole in front of us when it comes to assuring the security operation of this new platform. If regulators wait, it will be more challenging to govern Metaverse once there is a higher level of user dependence, thus they must act now, while Metaverse is still in its infancy, before the technology advances. Although disruptive technologies like VR, AR, blockchain, etc., have enormous potential in their applications, there is still doubt over how they will affect established legal systems. It goes without saying that regulating new technologies would be challenging and would call for a revision of current legal frameworks.

<u>Author's Bio</u>

Duvvuru Sravya Reddy is a 3rd year BBA LLB student at IFIM LAW SCHOOL, BANGLORE. She is interest in Criminal law and laws relating AI and information technology. She has her internship experience in blog writing. She has also interned with Adv. C Raghu in HIGH COURT FOR THE STATE OF TELANGANA.

CHAPTER EIGHT

ANALYSIS OF MISFEASANCE AND NONFEASANCE IN THE LIGHT OF DONOGHUE & STEVENSON

Author: Abhinav Singh, II year of B.A.,LL.B.(Hons.) from Marwadi University

INTRODUCTION

Donoghue v. Stevenson was one of the land mark judgment, not only in England but all over the world as it had not only safeguarded the rights of the peoples but also expanded the scope, flexibility and provided some stability to the tort law, which till date is confusing. Also known as snail in the bottle case had proved that if we will try to confine the tort only to some definitions, then it will curtail the rights of the consumers and will provide a freehand to the manufactures to escape, from almost every liability. Stevenson (Manufacturer) had won the case in lower courts, and this was the case filed under the appellant jurisdiction of the House of Lords (Division bench) UK. The case was mainly based upon the liability of the manufacturer, as the rights of the consumer got affected by the negligence on the part of the respondent (Stevenson) by consuming the article manufactured by the respondent. There were many questions in front of the bench, which will be discussed later, but one of the important question raised that there was no direct relation between the respondent and the consumer and due to this reason respondent does not have any responsibility towards appellant. This has also created a confusion regarding duty towards third person. Although at the end, the judgment was delivered in the favour of appellant by the majority of 3:2.

CONCEPT OF BREACH OF DUTY

Breach of duty is one of the necessary requirements for a person to be held accountable for carelessness. In legal filed it means someone failure to perform or performance of any act prohibited by law. It indicates that when executing an act, everyone owes a responsibility of care to another person. Although this obligation occurs in all activities, it is legal in nature in carelessness it can't be moral, ethical, or religious in nature. The court will compare the defendant act with the act a common reasonable prudent man would taken in the same situation and if the court find out that the defendant have acted unreasonably then the defendant will be held liable. The concept of breach of duty was much debated in Donoghue v. Stevenson. The company tried to prove that the breach of duty on their part noting the fact that the breach can only occur when there is any contract between the parties and the person who purchased the drink does not have any contract with the company. But the court held that if the commodity is of type that it is impossible for the purchaser to check the ingredients of the product then the purchaser can claim the breach of duty under negligence. It was said by Lord Atkin in Appeal that main question before the bench is to find out, that whether there was negligence on the manufacturer part and breach of duty occurred or not. Under law of tort a person has to vigilant regarding the rights of every person in the society and need to take due care towards all the persons in a society. In this case although the person consuming the drink was not in direct contract with the manufacturer but the manufacturer need to take due diligence in manufacturing the drink as the person consuming could face serious risk because of the manufacturer and it will affect the right of the consumer because of the negligence of the producers. So breach of duty means, that the negligence have caused the legal damage to the party. In order to prove breach of duty in negligence you need to prove that the party owed the duty of care towards another and the party has breached their duty and that breach has caused legal damage to the plaintiff. The main part in breach is prove that the negligence that occurred could have been avoided, if the defendant would have taken ordinary diligence, which any reasonable person would take in order to execute the work.

Explaining the view taken by the lord Esher in Heaven v. Pender, that duty to take due care did arise when the person or property of one was in such proximity to the person or property of another that if due care was not taken damage might be done by the one to the other[1]. This does not mean that the truth of proximity is only confined to the physical proximity, but be applied to the extent that the act of one party may directly affect a person whom the alleged person is bound to take care would know would be directly affected by his careless act.[2]. It is also evident from the observation of lord Esher and A.L. Smith in Le Lievre v. Gould, 1893, 1 Q.B. 497, Lord Esher at p.no 497 says,

"That case established that under certain circumstances one man may owe a duty to another even though there is no contract between them. If one man is near to another or is near to the property of another a duty lies upon him not to do that which may cause a personal injury to that other or may injure his property"[3]. The other important principle is the necessity of goods having to be used immediately or there is a reasonable time for the consumer to inspect it before consuming, as it give rise to the deterioration of goods by lapse of time or the intermediate person could also have at fault. And then the manufacturer may does not have the liability, but if the manufacturer puts the goods in container knowing the fact that it will be directly opened by the consumer and there can be no inspection by any purchaser and negligently by not taking due care the manufacturer allows the goods to filled with poison or any other material which should not have been in the product, and then the aggrieved party does not have any right or remedy against the negligent act of the manufacturer would cause great injustice to the aggrieved party and will be very dangerous for all the consumers and will provide a free hand to all the manufactures to escape their liability, citing the principle of no contract with the consumer. Especially In the cases of house hold products, where the manufacturer have the clear knowledge that the product will be used by the other persons that the actual purchaser and by the member of the family, it should be the liability of the manufacturer.

In the case of George v. Skivington, where the defendant was the shampoo manufacturer and the plaintiff brought the bottle of shampoo to be used by his wife, and the product was manufactured so negligently that it was totally unfit for the use and because of this the female plaintiff was injured. The justice Kelly C.B said that there was no question of warranty but whether the chemist was liable in an action on the case for unskilfulness and negligence in the manufacture of it; "Unquestionably, there was such a duty toward the purchaser and it extends in my judgment to the person for whose use the vendor knew the compound was purchased.[4]

So if the manufacturer is negligent in his/her act and does not take due care and that act leads to the breach of duty towards plaintiff and his/her right have been affected, then the defendant will be held liable.

Relation between Breach of Duty and Misfeasance and Nonfeasance

Misfeasance in tort law- It means "performance of some lawful Acts in an improper way". The Act is legal but has been performed in an improper way. It can be infer that there was negligence on the part of the person in performing the lawful Act.

Nonfeasance on the contrary means an intentional failure to perform a required duty, so if the person negligently omits or Act in a way he/she should not have been acted then that Act of the person will come under Nonfeasance. So for example in a case where a builder got a contract to build a factory and he also obtained the clearance for the same by the inspectors, now later as the base of the factory was not strong, that structure collapsed. Now in this example the inspectors who cleared the documents without checking it will be termed as Misfeasance and the builders who have build the factory will come under Nonfeasance as they were directly negligent in their act on the contrary the inspectors were negligent in performing the lawful task.

The breath and the extent of the neighbour principle in Donoghue v. Stevenson have made it difficult to identify the difference between Misfeasance and Nonfeasance. A s the neighbour principle which came out of the judgment setup a very broader benchmark to decide the liability of a person towards others so it became too difference that whether the breach will come as negligent act performing an lawful act or an negligent act in itself.

It was also a contention that the amount of liability attached with the Misfeasance is difficult to decipher as the person is not legally bind to perform that act. Suppose an individual is witnessing a crime in front of him and there are other people present then the person can informs the police but if he chooses to not to inform then why blame this person by bringing the claim of negligence as there can be various reasons for which he do not want to perform the police so we can say that it was not really the duty of the person attached with him, but as the neighbour principle suggested it was the duty of the person to inform the police as it is in the ambit of the definition of neighbour.

To identify the scope of the legal duty the Lord Atkin have quoted a passage from the Book of Luke is a parable of the good Samaritan who stopped to assist a wounded man after a priest and a Levite had walked past but crossed to the other side. The consensus is that Lord Atkin meant to explain is that despite the immorality of the priest and the Levite those men would not be legally liable.

CONCLUSION

The judgment provided in the Donoghue v. Stevenson had taken into consideration the fact that if the product of the manufacturer is directly affecting the rights of the consumer and the consumer do not have any mechanism to check that fact then the principle of Neighbour will be active and the manufacturer will be held liable. However the judgment have reduced the differentiation between the concept of Misfeasance and Nonfeasance and it had made it very difficult for the courts to decide the amount of negligence and breach an individual had done and it would lie in which category.

As a result, Donoghue v. Stevenson effectively establishes a criterion for duty of care. However, as legal turbulence grew, the stated criterion became overly simplistic. In Caparo Industries Plc v. Dickman, a three-step neighbour test was created (1990) to reduce that misconceptions and confusions. The exam, on the other hand, was founded on Lord Atkin's original idea. This approach has been further refined in other circumstances.

Many academics, however, reject the ongoing hype around this case, claiming that the concepts presented are too simple. However, it is for this reason that the author considers that a thorough examination of the case law is required. As instances get more complicated, it is acceptable to say that a significant need to return to the basics and study all those that are now taken for granted.

There have been some judgments which have tried to explain the principle of Donoghue v. Stevenson in a more elaborative way, considering the current circumstances of the society. They have also tried to be less confusing, but the significance of the snail case has not reduced as its significance can be seen as it have been cited by the Hon'ble supreme court of India in its recent judgment of The Managing Director, Kerala Tourism Development Corporation Ltd. v. Deepti Singh and Ors. (2019), which clearly proves that the principle of that case are still prevalent and are still acting as a guiding force for various Courts to come to a conclusion.

From the time of the judgment the society has developed and as per the changes, the law has also broadened the scope of the duty owned towards others. The section 2(7) of the Consumer protection Act, 2019 has expanded the definition of the consumers as the person, who does not necessarily purchase the goods and services, but also who consume the goods and services will also be termed as consumer and will have all the right to sue the manufacturer. As, according to the previous definition of the consumer, person who had purchased the goods can only file a suit against respondent for any damage, which curtailed the rights of lot of consumers as they were the once directly affected by the negligence of the manufacturer. Section 2(5)(f)(g) of the Act also giver the right to legal heirsor legal representative to file a suit in consumer protection and allows a guardian to file on the behalf of his/her child. These definition have been in consonance with the judgment that whosoever, purchases the goods or avail any service for the end use and whoever take benefit or consumes it have the right to claim compensation. This have created a proper check and balances upon the supplier of goods and services to make sure that every due diligence have been taken care off. The Act itself was based upon the various landmark judgments, which have been very important for the rights of the consumers.

CHAPTER NINE

One Nation, One Exam: A comfort or just another distress

Author: Rashika Mathur, III year of B.E. Electrical from Dr . Kiran Pallavi Global University (affiliated to Gujarat Technological University)

We all have given entrance or eligibility exams at some point in life, let aside whether it is a public or private university. Have you ever thought that just giving a unified exam and you will get your university according to your preference of profession?

University Grant Commission (UGC) all the way has come up with a proposal to merge National Eligibility Entrance Test (NEET) for Medical Colleges and Joint Entrance Exam (JEE) for IITs, NITs, IIITs etc. into Common University Entrance Test (CUET). Moreover, in a recent interview with Times of India, Chairman of UGC, M Jagdesh Kumar, clarified various things regarding this.[i]

There are diverse views among students regarding this proposal of UGC; some defend this proposal by stating that it will reduce burden, and some oppose saying that it will be a blunder on account of logistics failure which is new normal during such Examinations.

What did the Chairman of UGC state?

M Jagdesh Kumar was very reluctant to accept logistics failure during CUET's last phase and defended it by saying that National Testing Agency is in the learning stage. All ambiguities are being taken care of. Speaking on the one nation exam, he stated that the proposal is ready, and students need not worry as UGC is in no hurry to implement it; there will be proper consultation and planning. He supported this proposal by saying that this step reduces the burden on students.

He seems to tranquillize the critics with the promise of the expert committee on this subject matter and also stated that stakeholders know about the enigma around this proposal and that everything will be addressed appropriately.

<u>What merits could it bring to students and the Government across the nation?</u>

In my opinion, this step will surely simplify the process of selecting a Government University and College; if we talk about today's scenario, the examination process is too complicated, and students who have the guidance of someone quickly learn the way. However, students from remote areas find learning about these mainstream diversified exams challenging and lose many times. However, if this proposal gets a green flag, everyone will have to focus on one exam after their 12th exam.

Moreover, as per UGC, this unified exam will take place twice a year[ii]Students will have another chance if their phase- 1 does not go well. In my opinion, these 2- phase examinations will help students hold on to their hopes and considerably reduce the number of suicide cases in India. According to NCRB, every day, 28 students attempt suicide in India, which is a deplorable state of affairs[iii]. And out of 100%, 1.4% people commit suicide due to 'Failure in examinations[iv]. It may sound less but think about the grief and sorrow they leave behind for their ageing parents. This step will significantly help students not to take such steps.

It will be easier for the Government to consider earnings and expenditure from such exams. For example,according to an RTI, NTA made whooping 192 crores and saved 155 crores after expenditure on exam conduction and counselling in 2019. [v]Imagine the numbers that Government earns from all such competitive exams. If this proposal gets accepted, it will save man force and resources for accounting and collecting such a massive amount of money. Additionally, Government will earn more interest on the principal amount.

<u>Why are students criticizing this proposal?</u>

After news came out that such a proposal was under consideration, students were divided into appraisers and criticizers; if we look at this proposal critically, yes, there are many loopholes that are to be worked out and will not be easy peasy.

A section of students is worried that this will take more toll on mental issues than anything else, as this proposal put them in a do-or-die situation.

Until now, there is ambiguity over how many chances a student will have to give this unified exam.

Though the UGC chairman assured us that there would be proper consultation and planning before implementing this proposal, as we all know, this Government is famous for executing decisions without proper planning, recent example: Demonetisation etc. It is a matter of worry for students across the nation, 'Will this government properly plan before implementing this proposal?' Because it is a well-known fact that the difficulty level and syllabus are not the same for any of the two exams.

There is dissent among students regarding the Logistical and facilities needed to conduct this exam. Logistical failure during CUET phase- 1 has increased frowning lines overhead students. Does Government have human resources and management so good that students will not suffer? Chairman hinted that UGC is planning to implement it next year. Students are just asking a question, 'Is the government ready to conduct this big exam in ground reality anytime soon?' If you ask this question, my answer would be no.

Someone who has absolutely no objection to this proposal?The answer is Private Universities; students claim that this proposal puts privately owned universities into a win-win situation. Those who want admission desperately after failing this unified exam will be lured by Private Universities, which will demand high fees and take a toll on the pocket of guardians. We are still recovering from damage incurred by COVid-19, specifically financial loss faced by the middle- class of India; amid this, no parent wants his or her ward to stop studies. So, they will do whatever they can to make her ward study in the best colleges and universities. Privately owned firms will take advantage of this situation.

The learning gap is a real thing in India, which this proposal will widen. Tier- 1 and Tier- 3 cities not only have a vast development gaps but also learning gaps. In my opinion, it will be widened if this proposal passes. Tier- 3 cities still lack basic facilities; the learning gap is inevitable to resist.

<u>Author's honest opinion</u>

First, I would like to quote Nelson Mandela, "Stop being afraid of what could go wrong and think of what could go right." Things may seem complicated initially, but if I talk personally, I belong to an exceptionally far place, and there was no one to guide me about what exam to attempt and how to attempt it. However, somehow I managed to do it myself. When I think of other students, I feel pretty bad about how complicatedthis entrance examinations system is; how many students lose opportunities to this? In my opinion, this is a good initiative by UGC and Government, but ambiguities must be taken care of properly. So students should not suffer in any case.

<u>Author's Bio</u>

Rashika Mathur, 3rd a year Engineering student from Gujrat Technological University. A socio-legal activist, voicing opinions through articles and blogs.

CHAPTER TEN

SEDITION; AMEND, NOT SCRAP

Author: Shreyash Dube, I year of BA.LLB(Hons) from National Law University, Sonepat

Section 124A of the Indian Penal Code (Sedition) has been a subject of intense debate since our nation's inception and Constitution. Certain developments in recent times have only served to excite further the discussion surrounding this topic. On April 27, The Supreme Court heard two petitions filed by retired Army general S.G. Vombatkere and the other by the Editors Guild of India. Both the petitions were seeking to quash Section 124A. On May 11, Section 124A was put in abeyance by the Supreme Court until the Government could complete its review. Advocate General K.K. Venugopal and Solicitor General Tushar Mehta represented the Government. It earlier argued to maintain the status quo but later shared the Centre's plan to get rid of colonial baggage.

The core provision of this highly controversial law reads as follows; "Whoever, by words, either spoken or written, or by signs, or by visible representation, or otherwise, brings or attempts to bring into hatred or contempt, or excites or attempts to excite disaffection towards, the Government established by law shall be punished with imprisonment for life, to which fine may be added...."

Those opposing Section 124A primarily seek its abolishment along with overruling the Kedarnath Judgement. TheKedarnath Singh vs. State of Bihar (1962)is the leading authority when dealing with cases related to sedition. It infamously upheld the constitutionality of Section 124A. The opposition often relies on specific recurring arguments, which include but are not limited to ;

1. The colonial past of the sedition law and its use against our freedom fighters.

2. The word 'sedition' was dropped from the Constitution by the constituent assembly.

3. Sedition is antithetical to the spirit of dissent in a democracy.

4. The low conviction rates under sedition law and finally,

5. The existence of alternative laws.

This blog attempts to refute some of the most common arguments used against sedition and try to provide an alternative remedy for the same.

Sedition and Intent of the Constituent assembly

Many rely on K.M. Munshi's amendment, which resulted in the term 'sedition' being dropped from the initial drafts of the Constitution, to argue that the constituent assembly never intended to criminalise sedition or restrict speech based on it. Munshi is often quoted as saying that "the essence of democracy is criticism of the government." However, this is nothing short of selective interpretation. Though K.M. Munshi was an advocate of freedom of speech, he also understood the importance of the security and stability of the State. In his own words, "where Government and the law ceases to be obeyed because no respect is felt any longer for them, only anarchy can follow ."He argued that there are two distinct interpretations of the word sedition. The first one, as understood at the time IPC was enacted, could penalise mere processions or meetings or even a critical opinion against the British Government. The second definition, as it was understood in 1942, included offences against the State, including those through illegal and violent means. The intent behind Munshi's amendment was to provide a better phraseology, to move away from the first definition and closer to the latter interpretation. As Munshi himself stated, "This amendment therefore seeks to use words which properly answer to the implication of the word 'Sedition' as understood by the present generation in a democracy and therefore there is no substantial change." Though the word 'sedition' was replaced by the words which "undermines the security of, or tends to overthrow, the State," The essence of the crime of sedition was never removed from the Constitution. This idea of security of the State and the need to protect it from anarchy is the same rationale underlying the Kedarnath Judgement.

Colonial Government vs. Government Established by Law

Critics of sedition view it as a vestige of India's colonial legacy. They quickly point out how this law was used to persecute India's freedom fighters, suppressing their voices of dissent. The most notable names trialled under sedition pre-independence include Mahatma Gandhi and Bal Gangadhar Tilak. However, such critics often overlook that the Government established under British rule is not the same as the Government of India in power today. That is, an entity established by foreign invaders and colonisers is not the same as a democratically elected government which is the legitimate voice of the people of India. A government elected by the people is an expression of the will of the people. A straightforward question to ask ourselves then is, Does the legitimate voice of the people of India not deserve protection against illegal attempts to overthrow it ?. The Kedarnath Judgement of 1962 notes that the State manifests itself as the Government established by law' (symbol of the State).Further noting that " The very existence of the State will be in jeopardy if the Government established by law is subverted." The provision for sedition is simply a way for the Government to maintain law and order and ensure its safety against violent and illegal revolutions. Such attempts to violently and illegally overthrow the Government are at odds with the democratic principles of the Indian State.

Sedition and Freedom of Speech, Dissent

Another accusation against Section 124 A is against the right to voice dissent. This includes criticism of the Government and its policies. However, looking at the provision and the existing judicial precedent, it is abundantly clear that sedition is not at odds with the right to criticise the Government. The Kedarnath Judgement demarcated the difference between what can be considered criticism and what can be penalised as seditious. The court, in its judgement, noted that " Comments, however strongly worded, expressing disapprobation of actions of the Government, without exciting those feelings which generate the inclination to cause public disorder by acts of violence, would not be penal." The individual is, therefore, free to criticise the Government and its policies and even call for a change in the ruling party by lawful means, such as through elections. The Judiciary has stood by the guidelines established by the Kedarnath judgement and vehemently protected the right to criticise. In the Vinod Dua case, a journalist was charged with sedition for making a Youtube video criticising the Government's Covid policy. While quashing these charges, the court extensively cited the Kedarnath judgement and noted that "Every journalist is entitled to the protection under the Kedar Nath Singh case (which defined the ambit of the offence of sedition under Section 124A

IPC)." In Kedar Nath Singh (1962), five judges of the Supreme Court made it clear that "allegedly seditious speech and expression may be punished only if the speech is an 'incitement' to 'violence,' or 'public disorder.'"

The protection to freedom of speech provided under the Kedarnath case is not limited to free and fair criticism. In the case of Balwant and Anr vs. State of Punjab (1995), two men were investigated and tried for sedition. The men had allegedly raised several questionable slogans such as 'Khalistan Zindabad,' 'Raj Karega Khalsa,' 'Hinduan Nun Punjab Chon KadhKeChhadange', 'Hun Mauka Aya Hai Raj Kayam Karan Da'. Such comments are distasteful and offensive. They do not qualify as legitimate criticism or dissent. Despite the nature of the slogans, the apex court still protected freedom of speech and expression. Noting that stray slogans raised by one or two individuals do not result in incitement of violence does not qualify the threshold for sedition as prescribed by the 1962 ruling. Such cases make it abundantly clear that Section 124 A is not against free speech or the right to voice dissent. It begs the question of whether the Kedarnath judgement deserves the negative image it has garnered as of late.

Sedition and Low conviction rates

This brings us to a very legitimate concern. The data released by the National Crime Reports Bureau (NCRB) points to an alarming increase in arrests made under sedition while the conviction rates lie at a startling 3 percent. These numbers indicate rampant misuse of the sedition law. Though one may be tempted to blame the provision itself for this trend, to hold the law itself responsible would be a case of misdiagnosis. To put this point into perspective, let us take the example of Section 498A or the Dowry Law. Despite amounting to approximately 30 percent (1.1 Lakh Cases)of all the cases registered under crimes against women, the conviction rate for the same lie at a measly 12 percent. However, to suggest that the same provision must be scrapped would be disastrous. Another law in this category is The Protection of Children from Sexual Offences Act, 2012. Though the legislation was drafted with good intent, The courts have repeatedly noted the propensity of this law to be misused. The solution, in this case, is not to repeal these laws but instead to amend these laws and minimise the possibility of misuse. Pointing out low conviction rates is not an argument against the law but its enforcement by those in power.

Alternative to Sedition

The last and final argument against sedition is the existence of alternative laws. proposing that since the IPC and Unlawful Activities

Prevention Act have provisions that penalise "disrupting the public order" or "overthrowing the government with violence and illegal means".There is no need for Section 124A. However, arguing for UAPA to repeal sedition would be catastrophic. First of all, UAPA has virtually been made the same as sedition. UAPA's Section 2(o)(iii) describes unlawful activity in relation to individual/association as follows ;

"[A]ny action taken by such individual or association (whether by committing an act or by words, either spoken or written or by signs or by visible representation or otherwise) ... (iii) which causes or is intended to cause disaffection against India."

The similarities to section 124 A can not go unnoticed with respect to the use of the word 'disaffection' or the description of an action that includes words, signs, or visual representation.

Moreover, the deletion of sedition while keeping UAPA would benefit the union government immensely. The State governments can use the sedition law without interference from the Union government. In effect, This allows the opposition-ruled state parties to arrest supporters of the national ruling party. On the other hand, Section 45 of UAPA states that no court shall take cognizance of any unlawful activity offence without the Central Government's previous sanction. Hence, in the absence of sedition where only UAPA remains, the Union Government will enjoy an unchallenged monopoly while taking away the same power from states ruled by the opposing party. This can also explain the change of heart that the union government had, which earlier defended sedition only to now oppose it. It can also be observed that Advocate General K.K. Venugopal referred to the misuse of sedition in reference to the Hanuman Chalisa case, Where two independent MLAs were arrested by the state government under the opposition's rule, No such comments were made about the Government's own alleged misuses.

The Next Step

To scrap Section 124A would be akin to throwing the baby with the bathwater. There is sufficient judicial precedent and intent on the part of the constituent assembly to justify the presence of sedition laws. The best way to shield the law from misuse would be to amend the language to ensure greater clarity. There needs to be more awareness and accountability on behalf of the police. To ensure a more productive and solution-oriented approach, we must strive for balance and avoid extreme positions of either inaction or overcorrection.

CHAPTER ELEVEN

FREEDOM OF SPEECH AND EXPRESSION VIS-À-VIS CONTEMPT OF COURT- NEED FOR BALANCE

Author: Kanishka Sharma, III year of B.A.,LL.B. from Symbiosis Law School, Hyderabad

Abstract

Humans express themselves in multiple ways like writing, speaking, dressing, pictures, etc. Freedom of speech was first established in the First Amendment of the United States Constitution in 1791. However, these speeches and expressions may hurt the sentiment of some other person.

It leads to the rise of conflict between people. Therefore, few restrictions have been imposed on people to avoid a chaotic situation. One of them is 'contempt of court.' The judicial system is one of the pillars of society. It further gave rise to the question if one can criticise the judicial system or its decisions. This clash has been observed in different cases. The paper glance over the origin of the concept of contempt of court and its need. Further, the bone of contention between freedom of speech and expression and contempt of court will be analysed. Various cases are looked over, along with the need for balance between the two. At last, the paper provides a conclusion and suggestions. The research methodology followed for the article is non-doctrinal. Sources like books, articles, cases, statues, etc. would be used for research.

Introduction

Freedom of Speech and Expression means the right to express one's views and beliefs freely through vocal, written, pictorial mode, etc. It is a fundamental right bestowed upon citizens of India by the constitution under article 19(a)[1], but it is not an absolute right. Freedom of Speech and Expression has certain reasonable restrictions along with it that it shall not "affect the operation of any existing law, or prevent the state from making any law, insofar as such law imposes reasonable restriction on the exercise of the right conferred by the said sub-clause in the interest of the sovereignty and integrity of India, the security of the State, friendly relation with foreign States, public order, decency or morality or in relation to contempt of court, defamation or incitement to an offence".[2]

Contempt of Court is defined in the Contempt of Court Act, 1971 under section (2)[3]. It states that: "(a) 'contempt of court' means civil contempt or criminal contempt; (b) 'civil contempt' means willful disobedience to any judgement, decree, direction, order, writ or other process of a court or willful breach of an undertaking given to a court; (c) 'criminal contempt' means the publication (whether by words, spoken or written, or by signs, or by visible representation, or otherwise) of any matter or the doing of any other act whatsoever which--(i) scandalises, or tends to scandalise, or lowers or tends to lower the authority of, any court; or(ii) prejudices, or interferes or tends to interfere with, the due course of any judicial proceeding; or(iii) interferes or tends to interfere with, or obstructs or tends to obstruct, the administration of justice in any other manner;(d) 'High Court' means the High Court for a State or a Union territory, and includes the court of the Judicial Commissioner in any Union territory." [4]

The act doesn't only provide power to courts to try people for 'Contempt of Court' but also offers general defenses for people to restrain arbitrary use of this power by courts. Few defenses available are under section (4) "Fair and accurate report of judicial proceeding not contempt" [5], section (5) "Fair criticism of judicial act not contempt" [6], section (13) "Contempts not punishable in certain cases.—Notwithstanding anything contained in any law for the time being in force,— (a) no court shall impose a sentence under this act for a contempt of court unless it is satisfied that the contempt is of such a nature that it substantially interferes, or tends substantially to interfere with the due course of justice; (b) the court may permit, in any proceeding for contempt of court, justification by truth as a valid defence if it is satisfied that it is in public interest and the request for invoking the said defence is bona fide" [7], etc. The truth was introduced as a defense after the case of "Indirect Tax Practitioners' Association v. R.K. Jain" [8], (2010).

The punishments for Contempt of Court are provided under this act. Under section 12[9] of Contempt of Court Act, 1971, "Sub section 1 says that 'a contempt of court may be punished with simple imprisonment for a term which may extend to six months, or with fine which may extend to two thousand rupees, or with both:' Provided accused may be discharged or the punishment may be remitted on apology being made to the satisfaction of the court. Sub section 2 says that 'no court shall impose a sentence in excess of that specified in sub section (1) for any contempt'. Sub section 3 deals with the discretion of the court on punishment; Sub section 4 deals with the punishment for the person found guilty of contempt of court in respect of any undertaking given to a court is a company; Sub section 5 says that where the contempt of court referred to therein has been committed by a company and it is proved that the contempt has been committed with the consent or connivance of, or is attributable to any neglect on the part of, any director, manager, secretary or other officer of the company, such director, manager, secretary or other officer shall also be deemed to be guilty of the contempt and the punishment may be enforced, with the leave of the court, by the detention in civil prison of such director, manager, secretary or other officer".[10]

There had always been a debate that article 19(a)[11] and contempt of court had always shared a relationwhich is of juxtaposition in nature. A lingering question that comes with it is at which point the freedom of speech and expression ends, and contempt of court starts; there are no clear lines. Different statements are open to varying interpretations by many people. Another problem accompanied by this issue is that if the court can use the power of contempt of court to stifle freedom of speech and expression? This problem calls for an action to maintain a balance between freedom of speech and expression vis-à-vis contempt to court.

An example of the blur lines between freedom of speech and expression and contempt of court and different interpretations would be the case of Mr. Prashant Bhushan, advocate. Mr. Bhushan was charged with criminal contempt of court for his tweets, undermining the dignity of the Supreme Court of India and shaking the public's confidence in the judiciary. He was given an option to apologize, but he denied it; thus, the court ordered him to pay Re. 1/- as a fine, and if he fails to do so by the specified date, then imprisonment for three months and a three-year ban from practicing in the particular court.

Origin and Need of "Contempt of Court"

The concept of contempt of court finds its roots in the notion of 'Contempt of King' in the Anglo-Saxon' Oferhyrnes.' According to the ' Laws ', the idea of 'Contempt of Justice' was also considered an offense in the first half of the 12th century. There is mention of 'Contempt of King's writs' and 'overseunessa', a fine for contempt or disregard of orders in 'Laws' of Henry I. However, we don't find any mention of the term 'contempt of court' in 'Consuetudines et Justicie' of 1091 AD or in 'Laws of Normandy .'Before the end of the 12th century, England recognized the expression' contempt of court' and applied it to people's wrongs. Normandy was under French Kings in the 13th century, where we find 'con/emfipus curiae' and similar things under the title of 'contemplus juslitiae'.

In the 13th century, the principles of punishments of contempt were laid down by Bacton. He also states that there is no greater crime for a subject than contempt and disobeying King and his officers. Magna Carta also has no reference to the word 'contempt,' and the earliest mention of this word was found to be in 'Stature of Labourers .'Later many specific offenses came under contempt with punishments.

The first half of the 18th century witnessed distinguish between 'contempt of court and 'contempt out of court' by Lord Selborne's classification by introducing the "Contempts of Court Bill" in 1883. India adopted contempt of court from the British due to being their colony. Contempt of Court Act, 1971[12] takes its basis from there.

The objective of establishing 'contempt of court' was to maintain the dignity and image of the court before the people. If any publication or act undermines the court's authority and trust in the justice of the court is shaken, then the offender needs to be punished. Maintaining the court's dignity is necessary for the faith of people in the judicial system; if that faith is broken, it will lead to a situation of havoc. People will have nowhere to go to get justice peacefully, leading to the public resorting to violent means for revenge for injustice done to them, leading to anarchy throughout the country. 'Contempt of Court' also helps in the smooth running of administration in courts without any unnecessary hurdles to serve justice to the victims as quickly as possible.

Bone of Contention

Article 19(1) (a)[13] provides every citizen the fundamental right of "freedom of speech and expression"; however, these rights are not absolute. Certain restrictions accompany this right given in Article 19(2). One of the restrictions is contempt of court. One can exercise their right of freedom of speech and expression till the time s/he is not committing contempt of court. This restriction was made to ensure the dignity of the court is maintained.

A person accused of criminal contempt of court is tried under the same court but with different judges than the report or verdict criticized. Now, India is a republic and democratic nation. It derives its power from the people and thus acts as a master to all institutions of India. The citizens shall have the right to criticize the institutions regarding their improper performance. However, that's not the case in the judicial system. A person publishing anything undermining the authority and dignity of the court is charged with contempt of court. It is the bone of contention between the fundamental right of freedom of speech and expression and criminal contempt of court.

Courts are often accused of using this power arbitrarily to stifle "freedom of speech and expression," thus violating the fundamental rights of citizens. It is said that courts assert their dominance by misusing this power, though some defenses exist like fair criticism and truth. A person accused of criminal contempt of court is tried under the same court, but different judges than the report or verdict criticized still it is court's discretion to charge one person with contempt of court. The court defends itself by saying that a person can criticize a Judge to the extent which doesn't hinder its working. It gives rise to another question is criticizing a judge and court the same thing or not? It is answered in the case of Brahma Prakash Sharma And Others v. The State Of Uttar Pradesh[14] where it was held "attack on individual judges or the court as a whole with or without reference to particular cases, casting unwarranted and defamatory aspersions upon the character or ability of the judges. Such conduct is punished as contempt for this reason that it tends to create distrust in the popular mind and impair the confidence of the people in the courts which are of prime importance to the litigants in the protection of their rights and liberties." [15]

Another criticism that 'contempt of court' faces is that people use it to gain publicity and come into the limelight. Mere statements that most people would ignore or look over are given unnecessary importance and waste the court's valuable time on trifle matters while delaying the justice for many other victims facing much more severe offenses. It was stated by Ms. Arundhati Roy, a famous writer, in Re: Arundhati Roy[16] where she states that "By entertaining a petition based on an FIR that even a local police station does not see fit to act upon, the Supreme Court is doing its own reputation and credibility considerable harm"[17].

Instances of Confrontation

Few cases attracted the public's attention on a large scale due to the tiff and vague line between freedom of speech and expression and contempt of court.

In the case of P.N. Duda v. V. P. Shiv Shankar & Others[18], Union Law Minister Mr.Shankar was not held guilty of criminal contempt of court. However, he stated "Anti-social elements i.e. FERA violators, bride burners and whole hordes of reactionaries have found their heaven in the Supreme Court". Another irony that accompanied it was similar to the speech of Kerela's Chief Minister, Mr. Nambudripad, who was held guilty for contempt of court. The justification given by Supreme Court was that Mr. Shankar had "special knowledge" regarding the field of Law, and the right to criticise court should be granted to educationally qualified people.

In Re: Arundhati Roy, the writer was held guilty under 'Contempt of Court' due to her statement, "It indicates a disquieting inclination on the part of the court to silence criticism and muzzle dissent, to harass and intimidate those who disagree with it" [19]. However, this decision attracted a lot of controversy with it. In the case of Brahma Prakash Sharma And Others v. The State of Uttar Pradesh, it was mentioned that 'degree of publicity' is a factor for deciding contempt of court. However, Ms. Roy made this statement in the affidavit, which is not a public document, thus attracting dissent from people that the statement wouldn't have made a public impact. Ms. Roy also stated that her comments are 'fair criticism' with proof and examples still Supreme Court didn't consider it due to her not being educationally qualified to do so.

Need for Balance

There is a need for balance between "freedom of speech and expression" and "contempt of court" for proper and impartial functioning of courts and for preserving the fundamental rights of India's citizens. They both are a need for a nation's growth and smooth functioning. "Freedom of speech and expression" provides a voice to people to speak their grievances but can be misused by evil-minded to misguide the public to create a state of anarchy. Similarly, contempt of court is a vital tool to ensure the smooth functioning of courts for the earliest delivery of justice to people. The absence of one of those will lead to an authoritarian or anarchical state. It would force people to live in a world full of injustice, where people are constantly in fear for their security and have no hope of peace.

Conclusion and Suggestion

The concept of "Contempt of Court" found its origin in Anglo-Saxon Laws. It came up as a necessary tool in the hands of rulers for control. After introducing fundamental rights, it stood in a contradictory position with "freedom of speech and expression." Both concepts were right at their places, having both pros and cons. The contradiction is witnessed in different cases, but a need for balance between the two came into existence.

The tiff between "freedom of speech and expression" and "contempt of court" is an important issue that needs to be resolved. It is the only way to bring out the best of both concepts without causing tension and dominance of one over the another. There is a need to overcome the vagueness and blurred lines accompanying these concepts for better working between them. Defining 'contempt of court' properly can be a way to avoid a problem like biases, arbitrary use of power, etc. It will help people know their restrictions better to avoid making statements under the purview of contempt of court and reduce the chances of abridging the fundamental right of "freedom of speech and expression."

Author's Bio

I am a third-year student at Symbiosis Law School pursuing a BA LLB degree. I am a member of the Literary and Debate Society of my college. I have participated in inter-college debates, national conferences, webinars, etc. I indulge in reading and writing also.

CHAPTER TWELVE

SOCIAL PERSPECTIVE OF LAW

Author: Princi Bhardwaj, pursuing B.A.LL.B (Hons.) from Aligarh Muslim University

Introduction

The Social Perspective of Law aims at studying the interrelationship between the law and society. It is concerned with understanding the actual working of laws by analyzing the functionals and practical aspects of law in a social set-up. The development and evolution of society did not happen in isolation and at a single place or time. The society evolved gradually and with its evolution several social, political and economic changes were also introduced. After the French Revolution of 1789, several social and economic changes came in the society.

As economic disparities grew among the people, the society began to be divided in various social classes which led to social inequalities. Individual rights and liberties began to be demanded by the people. With the introduction of such social and economic changes and the rise of modern science, social scientists realized the need of applying scientific methods to study the various aspects of law and society. In 1838, Auguste Comte, a French Philosopher, developed a new discipline called Sociology to study the various aspects of society. The introduction and development of Sociology as a discipline, led to the establishment of the Sociological School of Law. The Social Perspective of Law attempts to study the role of law in society and the application of various social sciences to the study of law so that Law can be used as a more effective instrument of social control and development. It wants to study the actual functioning of laws in society to achieve the common good of the people and to ensure that the laws that are made help in achieving the individual as well as the social interests. It aims at using law as an instrument to solve social problems. The chief proponents of this approach include Rudolf Van Ihering, Eugen Ehrlich, Roscoe Pound, Jeremy Bentham, Duguit etc.

The Social Perspective of Law aims at studying the interrelationship between Law and Society in the following four aspects:

1. Social Origin of Laws and Legal Institutions
2. Examination of impacts of law on society.
3. Inquiries regarding which laws should perform in society (Social Performance and tasks of Laws).
4. Test for validity of Laws.

Social Origin of Laws and Legal Institutions

According to the German philosopher, Rudolf Von Ihering, the origin of Laws takes place through Sociological factors.He defined law as a part of social conduct. Ihering believed that the primary necessity for law was to serve social needs and purposes. Laws should be able to serve the individual interests of people as well as the society as a whole. However, sometimes it becomes difficult to reconcile between the individual and social interests and the need for balance between various interests arises. For this purpose, those interests can be categorized into three kinds:

1. Individual Interest
2. Social Interest
3. State Interest

According to Ihering, such reconciliation of various interests can be brought through principle of the Levers of Social Motion. In this principle he combines the egoistic and altruistic motives of various interests through the Principle of Reward and The Principle of Coercion.

Principle of reward means awarding rewards in the process of legal framework if a person performs an altruistic act or honestly performs a duty that he is bound to do. This principle encourages people to contribute to social as well as economic welfare of the state.

Principle of Coercion means awarding the legal punishment if a person does an act which violates the legal or social norms or if he does not perform the duties which he was expected to do. This principle helps in maintaining the law and order of the state. It can further be divided into two categories:

1. Organized Coercion: It includes punishment for the violation of a legal duty or provision.
2. Unorganized Coercion:In this the punishment is given not for a legal wrong but for the violation of social norms and values. This type of Coercion can vary from one place to another depending on various factors.

Ihering defines the altruistic levers of social motion as the feelings of duty and love in which a person is not legally bound to do an altruistic act but he does so because of the feeling of love, respect and compassion. Ihering describes the feeling of love as a medium to achieve social ends and to peace, harmony and prosperity in society.

Ihering also talked about the interdependence of the various factors of society that are important to make the society functional. Ihering classified those factors into three categories:

1. Extra Legal Conditions: Those conditions which are under the control of nature.
2. Mixed Legal Conditions: Those conditions in which law does not play a significant role.
3. Purely Legal Conditions: Those interests which can be secured only by legal regulations.

Ihering considered law as "the sum of conditions of social life in the widest sense of the term, as secured by the power of the state through the means of external compulsion".[i]

Ihering is not in the favor of the priori theory of justice simply because of the reason that the laws which are considered to be bad today may be considered as good in the future as the social, economic and political conditions change because the social acceptance and successful implementation of laws mainly depend on the socio-economic conditions of the society.

Impacts of Law on Society

The impact of laws on various aspects of society is mainly explained by the theories and concepts given by the Jurist, Eugen Ehrlich. According to Ehrlich, the laws formed in formal legal Institutions such as statues, precedents, legislations etc. do not present a complete and adequate picture of what is actually happening in the community. The norms and values which actually govern the social communities are often quite different from the formal laws which sometimes exist only on the papers and not in reality. He made a distinction between Norms of Decision and Norms of Conduct.

The Norms of Decision represent the formal laws and correspond to the traditional knowledge and understanding of laws.

The Norms of Conduct represent the living law or the laws which actually govern the living norms of society or community.

Ehrlich explains that there is an inevitable gap between the Norms of Decision and the Norms of Conduct which means that the formally made laws do not always show the same impact on the ground or in reality as they do in the formal structure. It is often seen that laws do not get implemented to the level that they were intended to be when they were formally made.

To bridge this gap, Ehrlich gave the famous Theory of Living Laws.

The Theory of Living Laws:The jurist, Eugen Ehrlich gave the theory of living laws. According to Ehrlich the laws made by formal institutions do not present a true picture of the whole society as they are not uniformly implemented. According to Ehrlich, the living law of every society lies in the society itself and not in the formal legal Institutions. He was of the opinion that laws should not only be confined to the formal legal framework. It is important for the laws made for the benefit of society to be implemented in the actual social framework.

Awareness of the living law is very important for the effective functioning of laws. It is essential for the lawmakers to understand the ground reality of the laws after making them. A nexus and relation is important between the common people and the lawmakers because when there is no connection between the people (the ground reality) and the lawmakers, it leads to more confusion than solution.

Ehrlich considered the customs, morality and the practices of groups and associations as important factors in state control and regulation along with the formal laws of the state and its organs. He was of the view that Jurisprudence should not only be considered the formal laws or statues but it should also focus on the living law which plays an important role in regulating the society.

However, there were some drawbacks of Ehrlich's theory because of which it was criticized by jurists and social thinkers. His distinction between the Norms of Decision and the Norms of Conduct was accepted but he failed to explain the mutual interaction between the two. Also, he deprived the formal laws of any creative activity or usefulness and merely described them to be trailing behind the social developments.

Tasks of Laws in Society

The third aspect of Law that the Social Perspective of Law attempts to study is the tasks that laws are expected to perform in society. This aspect is mainly understood by the Utilitarian Theory of Jeremy Bentham, who is considered to be the pioneer of functional Jurisprudence.

The Utilitarian Theory:According to Jeremy Bentham, every man is governed by pleasure and pain and the purpose and function of laws should be to promote the greatest happiness to the greatest number of persons. This task of laws can be achieved through the Maximization of Pleasure and the Minimization of Pain. He also devised a method of measuring happiness through the quality of pleasure resulting from an action. The good actions resulted in pleasure while the bad ones resulted in pain. According to him, laws should aim at providing happiness, equality of opportunity and security for all the members of society. He favoured the acquisition of private property because he thought it to be important for the fulfillment of desires and expectations of people. He was of the view that laws should focus on the happiness of each individual which will gradually result in the happiness of the whole society and it will also promote justice, equality and well functioning of the laws in society. This theory asserted that the task of law making is to ensure the welfare of the people and to fulfill their needs and interests.

It also stated that laws should be judged according to their consequences.

Another significant proponent of Sociological Jurisprudence is Roscoe Pound. According to Roscoe Pound, the making, interpretation and application of laws should involve various social factors. To ensure this, he suggested that:[ii]

1. There should be a functional study of impacts of legal institutions on society.
2. There should be a social investigation before making the laws.
3. A constant study of law and society should continue to make the laws more effective on the ground level for which the Psychological and Sociological study of the Legal Methods and Legal History should be done.
4. Establishment of the Ministry of Justice to meet the social ends.

According to Roscoe Pound, in order to achieve the purpose of legal order, there must be:

1. Recognition of interests- individual, public and social.
2. A definition of the limits within which such Interests will be legally recognised and given effect to.
3. The security of these interests within the defined limits.

Using this classification as the basis of his theory, Roscoe Pound developed a famous theory of law which is called Social Engineering.

Social Engineering: The Theory of Social Engineering was given by Roscoe Pound. Social Engineering aims to make an efficient structure of society which requires the satisfaction of the maximum number of persons. It aims to achieve the maximum happiness and wants of the maximum people and to minimise the friction. This can be made possible by balancing the competing Interests of various groups. For this purpose Roscoe Pound has made a distinction between the individual, social and public interests.

Individual Interests

Individual interests are the wants and desires of an individual,and they are looked at from the point of view of an individual. Individual interest includes the following aspects:

1. Personality: It includes interests in the physical personality of a person, dignity, privacy, freedom of will, faith and belief, opinions and honor and reputation of a person.
2. Domestic Relations: Domestic relations of a person include his parents, children, spouse etc. Pound has made a distinction between the domestic relations of an individual and the social institutions of family and marriage.
3. Interests of Subsistence: These interests include the interest of acquiring private property, freedom of industry and contract, freedom of association and employment, having advantageous relations with others.

Public Interests

Roscoe Pound defined public interest as, ' the claims associated in title of a politically organised society; as one might say for convenience, the claims of the state, political organization of society'.[iii] In simple words, public interest can be defined as the demands and desires asserted by individuals from the point of view of the political or public life. It includes the:

- Interests of the state as a juristic person.
- Interests of the state as the guardian of social interests.

The Interests of state as a juristic person include:

- Liberty, integrity, freedom of actions and honour of the personality of the state.
- Claims of the politically organised society of the state.
- Recognition of state as the guardian of social interests.

Social Interests

Social Interests are the demands and desires of social life that are considered to be the claims of various social groups. Social Interests have dominance over the individual interests. Social Interests can be classified into the following six categories:

Social Interests in the General Society: These are the demands or desires asserted by the social groups in a civilized society. They are to be secured against those actions or forms of conduct which threaten the existence of the social groups. They include a number of factors such as- General Safety, General Health, Peace and Order, Security of acquisition and Security of Transactions.

Social Interests in the Security of Social Institutions: They include the demands or desires in a civilized society that the fundamental social institutions be secured from any form of action or conduct that threatens their existence or effective functioning. These institutions include- Social Institutions, Domestic Institutions, Political and Religious Institutions.

Social Interests in General Morals: It includes the demands or desires of society for the general security of the moral sentiments of the general public. It deals with sensitive issues like Prostitution, Gambling, Drunkenness and other unhealthy social practices.

Social Interests in the conservation of Social and Natural Resources: This principle of Roscoe Pound is similar to the modern day concept of Sustainable Development. Roscoe Pound asserted that the present generation of individuals should judiciously use the natural and social resources to fulfill their needs and desires so that the resources do not get exhausted. There should be no abuse of resources and they should be wisely used, keeping in mind the needs of the future generations also.

Social Interests in General Progress: This includes the demands and desires in a civilized society for human development and control over the natural and social resources to satisfy the human desires. It demands the continuous improvement in Social Engineering for the complete and higher development of human powers. These Interests are divided into three categories:

Economic Progress: It means the development of society in economic terms. It asserts that every member of society should be able to get the basic necessities and rights. It includes the freedom to use and sell property, Freedom of Trade and industry and encouragement of new and creative inventions by grant of patents.

Political Progress: It means that the basic rights and liberties should be available to every member of the society. It includes Freedom of Speech and Expression, Freedom of Association and the Freedom to assemble and protest peacefully.

Cultural Progress: Cultural Progress includes the promotion of Education, Art, Literature, freedom of science and learning and aesthetics.

Social Interests in Individual Life: It is concerned with the demands that each individual should be able to live according to the standards of society.

It includes self assertion, opportunity and conditions of life.

By drawing a distinction between the different kinds of Interests Roscoe Pound attempted to reconcile and balance between the conflicting interests of different members of society so that the purpose of law and order can be achieved.

<u>Validity of Laws</u>

This aspect of the Social Perspective of Law is concerned with the criterias to check the validity of Laws. It is mainly based on the works and theories of Leon Duguit. He made an attempt to develop an approach to the traditional concept of state and sovereignty and to study laws from the social perspective. This aspect is mainly based on Duguit'sPrinciple of Social Solidarity.

Principle of Social Solidarity: According to Duguit, the interdependence of humans is the most important and inescapable feature of human existence and society. He believes that all human beings are interdependent on each other since the very beginning of the society as it is impossible for humans to live in complete isolation. This interdependence becomes possible through the mutual cooperation among people as it leads to the smooth functioning of the society by promoting peace and harmony. This is the Principle of Social Solidarity.

According to Duguit, the state and its maintained institutions should be judged according to the contributions they make to promote social solidarity. Duguit also asserted that if the state fails to work for and promote social solidarity then it becomes the responsibility and duty of the citizens to revolt against the state. Duguit criticized the traditional concept of sovereignty of state. He held that the state is not indispensable and the legitimacy of his authority should be tested through the actions it performs in favor of social solidarity. He favored the sovereignty of the people and held that laws should be made according to the public needs and their opinions. According to him sovereignty can not exist if the interdependence, cooperation and peaceful existence of humans disappear.

He emphasized on the concept of Decentralization so that power does not stay in the hands of a single authority. He believed that Decentralization of power will lead to more accountable and more effective functioning of the government.

However, Duguit's Principle of Social Solidarity is the most ideal situation which is difficult to be achieved in the practical sense. For instance, the discriminations prevalent in society on various grounds are a hindrance in the promotion of social solidarity. Different laws should be made and affirmative actions should be taken to end such discriminations which will lead to social solidarity among the people. Duguit defined three types of forbidding laws that may help to promote Social Solidarity:

Freedom of Contract.

Respect for Property.

Liability only for fault.

According to Duguit, Social Solidarity is the valid criterion to test the validity of laws. Social Solidarity also makes people more obedient towards laws and strengthens their belief and trust in the legal system.

<u>Conclusion</u>

The Social Perspective of Law is concerned with the study of the interrelationship between Law and Society. It attempts to understand the actual functioning of laws in the social situations so that law can be used as an instrument of social control to meet the social ends. This Approach believes that the purpose of laws is to fulfill the needs and desires of the people. To ensure the fulfillment of this purpose, it attempts to study the relationship between law and society in four different aspects. The first aspect deals with the social origin of laws and legal Institutions according to which the eminent jurist, Ihering says that it is necessary to reconcile between the conflicting interests of different groups which can be achieved through the Principle of Levers of Social Motion which uses the Principle of reward and coercion for the maintenance of law and order in society.

The second aspect is the impact of laws on society which aims at studying how the laws affect the social conditions. This aspect is understood through the works of Eugen Ehrlich who gave the theory of living laws to understand the impacts of laws in society. According to this theory, the formally made laws should be properly implemented in reality also as sometimes the laws which exist on paper do not prove to be much effective in reality. Hence, the lawmakers should understand the social conditions and needs of the people before making the laws.

The third aspect is related to the performance of laws in society which is understood through the Utilitarian Theory of Jeremy Bentham and the Social Engineering Theory of Roscoe Pound. According to these theories laws are considered to be effective when they promote the happiness of the maximum number of persons and minimize friction. The Social Engineering Theory talks about the reconciliation of various kinds of interests to promote peace and harmony in society.

The fourth aspect is to check the validity of Laws in society which can be tested through the Principle of Social Solidarity given by Leon Duguit. According to this principle, the laws should promote social solidarity which leads to cooperation among people and helps in building a peaceful and harmonious community. All of these aspects are important to study the Social Perspective of Law which plays an important role in the effective functioning of Laws in society.

CHAPTER THIRTEEN

CYBERCRIME: BRIEF ANALYSIS

Author: Ankitha Thangamma K.U, pursuing BBA LLB(hons) from JSS law college, Mysuru, Karnataka.

INTRODUCTION

Cybercrime is not an ancient sort of crime to the world evolved. Cybercrime is one of the prevailing crimes playing a most devastating role in Modern India. Cyber Crime can be defined as criminal activity that takes place on or over computers and technological devices or the internet recognised by Information Technology. It is not only the criminals who are causing enormous loss to society or to the country but are also able to conceal their identity to escape from the clutches of the law.

The term "cybercrime" is being dealt with in The Information Technology Act, 2000; does not define the term cybercrime.Although, there are rulings provided by some Indian Courts about the terminology of cybercrime. Whatsoever good internet does to the growing world it equally has dark sides too. Cybercrime is becoming an intractable evil having its roots in the misuse of growing dependence on computers in modern life.

ORIGIN OF CYBER CRIME

Cybercrime is one of the modern issues. The story of cybercrime and security extends in the world back to 1970s. One of the very first versions of the internet was introduced, called theARPANET. Which has paved way for emergence of cyber security. This computer worm was revolutionary at the time when computer and messages were bouncing. It had no malicious intent. But, set a trend that explored the internet's vulnerabilities.

In the year 1980, the first ransomware attack was taken place. Again in the same year, Joseph Popp designed the AIDS Trojan to extort money, which was distributed on the floppy disk by door –to-door mail. An act was passed in the UK that made any unauthorised access illegal. Through this act, the foundation for cyber security protections was bought in the world which is amended even today. In 1992, the first cybercrime cases was seen which was Yahoo v. Akash Arora. [i]

DEFINITION

As mentioned in the introduction we have no particular definition provided in the Indian legislature. However, in general terms cybercrime means any illegal acts or activity taking place over the internet or through computers.

"The U.S. Department of Justice (DOJ) divides cybercrime into three categories:

1. Crimes in which a computing device is the target – for example, to gain network access;

2. Crimes in which the computer is used as a weapon – for example, to launch a denial-of-service (DOS) attack; and

3. Crimes in which the computer is used as an accessory to a crime – for example, using a computer to store illegally obtained data."[ii]

The convention of Europe Convention on cybercrime defines cybercrime as a 'wide range of malicious activities, including the illegal interception of data, systems interferences that compromise network integrity and availability, and copyright infringement".[iii]

CYBERCRIMINALS

Cybercrime is so rampant in day- to- day life that it is quite evident that any suspicious activity online may involve a cybercriminal. Before knowing the types, laws and preventive measures of cybercrime let us try to understand who cybercriminals are. Cybercriminals can be told as a person or a group of people who misuse technology to commit activities which are malicious on or over computers or any technological devices with the intention to obtain personal data through unauthorised access to generate profit

DOCTRINE OF MENS REA AND ACTUS REUS IN CYBERCRIME

As far as Traditional crime is concerned there are certain elements to constitute a crime. The elements of crime are human beings, mens rea, actus reus and injury. Mens rea means "guilty state of mind". There must be omission or commission to constitute a crime. And as far as actus reus is concerned, it means the omission of an act, by omitting to do something wherein the accused who is committing the crime so knows that he is prevented by law to do so. Actus reus in cybercrime has become a challenge as the crime or the act is being committed in a sophisticated environment. The person committing the act may leave footmarks on the computers or the device through which the cybercrime is taken place nonetheless it becomes a formidable task to be proved in the courts as evidence play a key role in every aspect of justice.

<u>TYPES OF CYBERCRIME</u>

1. CYBERSTALKING: Stalking in general sense means following the behaviours, actions or routine of an individual which impregnates fear. Cyber stalking is an extension of physical stalking which is taken place on or over the internet. Cyber stalker is a person who allegedly harasses an individual for purposes such as money, for love or any sexual reasons. The sources through which cyberstalking can be done are chat rooms, messages, voice mails, emails and spams are all options.

The Indian Information technology Amended Act, 2008 addresses the concept of cyber stalking under section 66A which runs towards the punishment for sending offensive messages through communication services

2. IDENTITY THEFT: Identity theft can be told as one of the most widest spreading cybercrime in the modern world.Identity theft means any person who obtains unauthorised personal information to steal money and gain access to private and sensitive information.

In the case, of BANK NSP CASE, the bank management trainee was engaged and was about to get hitched. The couple had exchanged plenty of mails using the company's computer. After a while, the couple broke up and the girl created false emails and started sending harassing emails to the boys' clients which resulted in a loss of boys clients and the company sued the bank. The bank was held liable for sending mails through its server.

3. PHISHING: This type of cybercrime is where the cybercriminals try to get in touch with individuals directly through phone or emails which lead to earning trust. They usually act as customer service employees to collect information regarding your name, bank account number and employer's name.

This is to trick people and reveal into revealing their identities and to have access to their personal information where they later sell these data to steal money.

4. SOFTWARE PIRACY: Software piracy is the act of stealing software programs with the intention of commercial or personal use. A person who carries out these acts of software piracy is called a software pirate. A

software pirate need not necessarily be an expert or a professional in programming, but a person with sufficient computer knowledge can also commit software piracy.

5. DATA DIDDLING: Data diddling is a type of cybercrime in which the data is altered before or while entering into the computer. Any person committing this act or who is involved in alteration, receiving, transmitting the data can be called as a cybercriminal. The consequences of committing this crime could be severe.

6. RANSOMWARE: In this type of attack the system is hacked and is under hostage until the victim pays the money which is demanded. Once the payment is done then the attacker provides the necessary details to gain control over the computer so targeted.

<u>PROCEDURE FOR REPORTING CYBERCRIME</u>

The Ministry of Home Affairs has come up with a tremendous platform which is named as the NATIONAL CYBERCRIME REPORTING PORTAL. The victim can file complaint according to their convenience either online or offline. The cybercrime complaint need not be filed in the place where the victim is residing but can be filed in any cybercrime cell. The victim can file or lodge FIR at the police station under section 154 of Code of Criminal Procedure.

➢ PROCEDURE FOR FILING CYBERCRIME COMPLAINT: OFFLINE: Making a written complaint to the cybercrime has been one of the most feasible ways wherein the victims can write the complaint which shall address the Head of the cybercrime cell. Any complaint that is to be filed must have information pertaining to the victim i.e. name, contact details and mailing address. Other documents which are required to be attached depend upon the complaint. It is necessary to attach these documents both online as well as with offline complaint.[iv]

➢ PROCEDURE FOR FILING CYBERCRIME: NATIONAL CYBER CRIME REPORTING PORTAL: With the emerging technology; the traditional methods are being overstepped. The cybercrime can be registered on National Cyber Crime Reporting Portal. Established by the Ministry of Home Affairs under the initiative of Government of India.

There are two types of complaint that can be registered on the National Cyber Crime Reporting Portal:

RELATED TO WOMEN OR CHILDREN: This may include any sexually explicit content that has been uploaded online, any material that contains explicit images of a child who is abused or exploited.

The complaint can be reported anonymously. The victim can follow the steps below

- Firstly, visit the website https://cybercrime.gov.in/
- Since this report is being filed anonymously the personal details of the victim need not be provided.
- The above mentioned crimes are only to be filed anonymously.
- The complaint must include with the suspects name and identity. It should also have details of the incident where and through which source it occurred. The residential address of the victim or where the crime was committed.[v]

The above mentioned, are the details and procedure that is to be mentioned while reporting the complaint by the victim. The victim can also attach additional documents and information that will be helpful for the investigation.

OTHER CYBERCRIMES: The victim or the complainant shall follow the following steps:

- Visit the website of National Cybercrime Reporting Portal.
- The complainant shall proceed to file the complaint on the portal by filling the necessary details.
- The contact number which has been given with the complaint; the complainant will receive an OTP which will be valid for 30 days.
- The complaint will be successfully registered.

<u>ANALYSIS OF CYBERCRIME IN INDIA</u>

The list of cybercrimes from the year, 2012 to 2021 are enlisted below;

2021 68,045

2020 50,035

2019 44,546

2018 27,248

2017 21,796

2016 12,317

201511,592

2014

9,622

2013

5,693

2012

3,477

As the above report, it is clear that there is an increase in the number of cybercrime from the year 2012-2021. The National Crime Record Bureau (NCRB) as per its latest data, reported 27,248

PREVENTIVE MEASURES

1. In order to prevent cybercrime make sure you do not disclose any of your personal information.

2. Always keep your computers updated with latest anti-virus software.

3. Do not send your credit card number or any of your bank details to any site that is not secured.

4. Using of firewalls may be helpful or beneficiary.

5. Keep a track of the site or apps which your children have been using in order to prevent any kind of harassment.

6. Make sure you have back up volume of data in order to prevent any kind of loses.

7. Using strong passwords.

8. Avoid opening of spam messages via emails or text messages.

These are few measures to be considered in order to prevent cybercrime.

LAWS GOVERNING CYBERCRIME

As mentioned earlier the laws relating to cybercrime is provided under theInformation Technology Act, 2000.

Section 65: Tampering with computer source documents.

It elaborates about the punishment and penalty for the crime committed by a person who knowingly or unknowingly destroys or alters any computer system. And the punishment for this offence is imprisonment for up to three years, or with both.

Section 66: Hacking with computer system.

Whoever commits an offence of hacking shall be punished with imprisonment up to three years, or with fine, or with both.

Section 67: Publishing of information which is obscene in electronic form.

Section 71: Penalty for misrepresentation.

Whoever makes any misrepresentation shall be punished with imprisonment or fine which may extend up to one lakh rupees, or with both.

Section 72: Penalty for breach of confidentiality and privacy.[vi]

As provided in this Act or any other law for the time being in force, any person who discloses any type of information, record, document or any material without consent shall be punished with imprisonment which may extend up to two years or with fine which may extend up to one lakh rupees or both.

The Information Technology Amendment Act 2008 also covers certain topics of cybercrime such as cybersecurity, cyber forensic and cyber terrorism.

CONCLUSION

Overall we have understood in depth that cyber crime is an intricate part of the modern day crime world and it is acknowledged that it doesn't show signs of reduction in the future. We have also understood that precautionary measures are necessary to protect ourselves from these crimes even though some cyber attacks may be beyond our control and also the due procedure to be followed to report them. Even though cyber crime investigation involves a lot of detailed investigation processes various police departments try solving them by raising cyber crime units and they are involved diligently in the investigation process

CHAPTER FOURTEEN

CORPORATE SOCIAL RESPONSIBILITY

Author: Kratika Khandelwal, B.Com., M.K.H.S. Gujarati Girls College, Indore, and institute of company secretaries of India

<u>Meaning</u>

corporate social responsibility is also called corporate citizenship or corporate responsibility. Generally ,CSR is understood to be the way forms integrated social ,environmental and economic concerns into their value culture decision making strategy and operations in a transparent and accountable manner and their by established better practices within the firm create wealth and improve society

<u>What exactly is the meaning of corporate social responsibility?</u>

As the name indicates it is the responsibilities that the corporates have towards society. Whenever we talk about corporate social responsibility always remember the words of Mohandas Karamchand Gandhi. In his works whatever funds the company has it belongs to the societies so company must strive that the funds should be used for the beneficial of society.

Corporate social responsibility is a strategy that looks at how the business can benefit the wider society. Firms engage incorporate social responsibilities for a number of reasons which includes :-

* Improving employee morale
* Better forms brand image
* Benefit the wider society

Corporate social responsibility is necessarily and evolving term that does not have a standard definition or a fully recognised set of specific criteria.

Corporate social responsibility is nothing but an organisation does to positively influence the society in which it exists. It could take the form of community relationship, volunteer assistant programmes, special scholarships, reservation of cultural heritage and beautification of cities.psychologically is basically to return the society what it has taken from it in the course reservations for the creation of wealth.

CSR is generally understood to be the way a company achieves a balance or integration of:-

* Economic
* Environmental and
* Social imperatives

Supreme court of India through a case study has defined the importance of corporate social responsibility. The case name is National textile workers v P.R.Ramkrishnan and the preservation 1983 SCR (1) 9

The supreme court of India ,in the case of National Textile Workers v P.R. Ramkrishnan and others 1983 SCR (1) 9 has encapsulated the whole genesis and significance of the concept of 'corporate social responsibility'.

" The concept of a company has undergone radical transformation in the last few decades. The traditional view of a company was that it was a convenient mechanical device for carrying on Trade and industry, Ameer legal framework providing a convenient institutional container for holding and using the powers of company management. The company low was at that time concieved merely as a statute intended to regulate the structure and mode of operation of a special type of economic institution called company.this was the view which prevailed for a long time in juristic circles all over the democratic world including United States of America, United Kingdom and India. Today social scientists and thinkers regard a company as a living vital and dynamic , social Organism with form and deep rooted affiliations with the rest of community in which it functions....A company according to the new social economic thinking is a social institution having duties and responsibility towards the community in which it functions.

Rule 2 (1) (d) of the companies (corporate social responsibility policy)

Corporate social responsibility means the activities undertaken by the company in persuons of its statutory obligation let down in section 135 of the act in accordance with the provisions contained in these rules but shall not include the following, namely:-

Activities Undertaker in persons of normal course of business of the company provided that any company engaged in research and development activity of new vaccine drugs and medical devices in their normal course of businessman Undertaker research and development activity of new vaccine drugs and medical devices related to covid-19 for financial year 2020- 21 , 2021-22,2022- 23 subject to the conditions that

(a) Search research and development activity shall be carried out in collaboration with any of the institutions or organisations mentionedin item (ix) of schedule VII to the Act;

(b) Details of search activity shall be disclose separately in the Annual report on CSR included in the board's report

- Any activity undertaken by the company outside India except for training of Indian sports personal representing any state or union territory at National level or India at international level;
- Contribution of any amount directly on indirectly to any political party under section 182 of the act;
- Activities benefiting employees of the company as defined in clause (k) of section 2 of the code on wages, 2019(29 of 2019)
- Activities supported by the companies on sponsorship basis for deriving marketing benefits for its products or services;

- Activities carried out for fulfillment of any other statutory obligation under any law in force in India.

This definition is the changed and expanded definition inserted by the companies (corporate social responsibility policy) Amendment Rules,2021 dated 22.01.2021 effective from 22ndJanuary 2021. This amendment has changed the entire rule regarding the definition.

CSR ACTIVITIES

CSR policy should be inconsistent with activities given under schedule VII of The Companies Act 2013:

A. Towards eradicating poverty, hunger and malnutrition, sanitation, and making available clean drinking water.

B. Promoting education, vacation skills, special education for children, women and elderly.

C. Promote gender equality, women empowerment, setting up old age homes, hostels, orphans, day care centers and other facilities for senior citizens and economically backward people.

D. Ensure sustainable environment, protection of flora and fauna, animal, soil, air water and all other natural resources.

E. Protect national heritage, art and culture, setting up libraries, protection and development of traditional art and handicrafts.

F. Measures towards Development of widows of armed forces people.

G. Promote rural sports, Olympics and Paralympic sports

H. Contribution towards prime minister national relief fund or any other fund set up by the central government.

I. Contribution towards research and development projects in the field of science technology or medicines.

J. Contribution to public funded universities, IITs, DRDO, AYUSH and ICMR etc.

K. Rural development projects.

CSR COMMITTEE

Companies that trigger any of the afforside conditions must constituted a corporate social responsibility committee of the board to formal letter monitor the CSR policy of the company. It is one of the first complaints is regarding CSR.

The companies (Amendment) Act, 2020 proposes to make the constitution of committee mandatory only where the CS are spend his more than rupees 50 lacs. This provision is made effective from 22nd January

2021.

The provision regarding constitution of the CSR committee is as follows

Listed companies – Three or more directors, out of which at least one shall be an independent director.

Unlisted public companies – Three or more directors, out of which at least one shall be an independent director.

However, if there is no requirement of having an independent director in the company, two or more directors

Private companies – Two or more directors. No independent directors are required as mentioned in the proviso under section 135(1)

Foreign company- At least two persons out of which :

1. one shall be the authorised person under section 380 of the act, and
2. another shall be nominated by the foreign company.

The board's report shell disclose the composition of the corporate social responsibility committee.

Functions of CSR Committee

- To formulate and recommend to the board, a CSR policy which would indicate the activities to be undertaken in areas or subject, specified in scheduled VII of the act
- To recommend the amount of the expenditure to be incurred on the activities undertaken in persons of the CSR policy.
- To monitor the CSR policy of the company time to time
- To formulate and recommend to the Board, and annual action plan in pursuance of its CSR policy

Schedule VII of companies Act,2013 describes the following activities to be undertaken as CSR :-

- Eradicate hunger, poverty malnutrition,
- Promoting education
- Promoting gender equalities
- Empowering women
- Setting up of homes and hostels for women, orphans
- Ensuring environmental sustainability ecological balance including contribution to the clean Ganga fund set up by the central government

for rejuvenation of river Ganga.
- Animal welfare
- Protection of national Heritage and culture
- Measures for benefit for armed forces, war windows and their dependent
- Training to promote rural sports.
- Rural development projects.
- Donating to floods
- Reducing child mortality
- Contribution to incubators or research and development projects in the field of science technology, engineering and medicine funded by the central government or State government or public sector undertaking or any agency of the central government of state government
- Slum area development
- Disaster management including relief, rehabilitation and reconstruction activities.
- However, in determining CSR activities to be undertaken, preference would need to be given to local areas and the areas around where the company operates.

NOTE: events, awards, charitable contribution, advertisement,sponsorship of TV program etc do not qualify as a part of CSR expenditure. The CSR activities are to be undertaken in project mode and not is a one-off projects

Ongoing projects

Ongoing projects is the new concept introduced under recent changes.

"Ongoing project" means a multi year project undertaken by a company in fulfillment of its CSR obligation having timelines not exceeding 3 years excluding the financial year in which it was commenced and shell include such project that was initially not approved as multi year project but whose duration has been extended beyond 1 year by the board based on reasonable specification

The following points are to be remembered

- Multi- financial year project (has an identifiable commencement and completion dates)
- Maximum period: financial year of commencement (when work order issued or contractfor execution awarded) + 3 financial years
- May not be approved as such but extended latter.

Important concept in case of transfer of unspent CSR amount (required to be made within 30 days of the end of financial year to a special account).

CSR policy relates to the activities to be undertaken by the company as a specified in scheduled VII of the act and the expenditure there on excluding activities undertaken in persuance of normal course of business of company.It is to be made actionable through the annual action plan

Corporate social responsibility applicability

As per section 135 of the companies act 2013, the CSR provision is applicable to companies which fullfils any of the following criteria during the immediately preceding financial year:-

- Companies having net worth of INR 500 crore or more, or
- Companies having turnover of INR 1000crore or more , or
- Companies having a net profit of INR 5 crore or , more.

Further, while calculating "net profit" following exclusions are required to be made

- Any profit arising from any overseas branch or branches of the company, whether operated as a separate company or otherwise; and
- Any dividend received from other companies in India, which are covered under and compliant with the provisions of section 135 of the act.

Net profit is required to be calculated as per provision of section 198 (which essentially makes it "profit before tax" and excludes capital payments/receipts)

MY OPINION ON CORPORATE SOCIAL RESPONSIBILITY

In my opinion, companies that follow up on corporate social responsibility are one-ways attract a large crowd of the public towards them. Because the leading companies have to dominate shareholding and that's because of the public who are contributing towards them. Directly or indirectly corporate social responsibility contributes not only to the betterment of society but the firm that fulfilling corporate social responsibility requirements and is telling the public that the motto of the company does not end at profit making but we even work for the best of our societies.

Whatever the corporate firms get is the trust of society so they should also maintain the same by contributing to today the leading firms are great examples of the same. These leading firms are even inspirations to those firms who are somewhere only seeing profit-making as their ultimate objective because they are losing people.

CHAPTER FIFTEEN

SHIFT FROM COMPETITIVE FEDERALISM TO COOPERATIVE FEDERALISM

Author: Anushmita Pramanik, B.A.LL.B (Hons) LL.M. from Ramaiah Institute of Legal Studies(Asst. Professor)

Introduction/federalism

The article studies the meaning of federalism in general terms. The rest of the paper tries to understand the federal features and the cooperative federal features in the political process of the country. The author tries to analyses the shift from rigid federalism to cooperative federalism and in this regard studies the legal framework and other measures that has strengthened the cooperative federalism in India.

Federalism is derived from a Latin word, 'foedus' meaning treaty, compact or contract. Federalism is "an indestructible union of destructible states" it was perceived that states must be integral part of India denying any right to Secede.[i] In this system powers have been divided between the two sets of government between the center and its constituent parts such as states or provinces.

There are two kinds of federations: -

1. Holding together federation – In this type, powers are shared between various constituent parts to accommodate the diversity in the whole entity. Here powers are generally titled towards the central authority. Example India, Spain and Belgicus.

2. Coming together Federation – In this type, independent states come together to form a larger unit. Here, states enjoy more autonomy as compared to the holding together kind of federation. Example USA,

Australia.

Federalism in India

India had emerged as an independent nation after a painful and bloody partition. Soon after independence, several princely states became a part of the country. The constitution declared India as a union of states. The constitution provided a threefold distribution of legislative powers between the union government and the state govt. Thus, it contains three lists.

1. Union list -includes subjects of national importance such as defense,foreign affairs, banking, communications and currency, we need a uniform policy on these matters throughout the country.

2. State list -includes subjects of state and local importance such as police, trade, commerce, agriculture and irrigation.

3. Concurrent list – forest, trade unions, marriage, adoption and succession. Both the union as well as the state government can make laws on the subjects mentioned in this list. If their laws conflict with each other, the law made by the Union Govt will prevail.

The sharing of power between the union government and the state government is basic to the structure of the constitution[ii]

Federalism with a strong Central Government

Indian constitution has created a strong central government, not only for strengthening the nation integrity of the nation but also to solve the socio-economic problems in the society. Important provisions that create a strong central government –

1. The parliament is empowered to form a new state by separation of territory from any state or by uniting two or more states. It can also alter the boundary of any states or even its name.

2. The constitution has certain very powerful emergency provisions, which can turn our federal polity into a highly centralized system once emergency is declared.

3. Even during normal circumstances, the central government has very effective financial powers and responsibilities. States are mostly depended on the grants and financial assistance from the center.

4. Besides, the governor has all the power to reserve a bill passed by the state legislature, for the assent of the president. This gives the central government an opportunity to delay the state legislation and also to examine such bills and veto them completely.

5. There may be occasions when the situation may demand that the central government needs to legislate on matters from the state list. This is

possible if the move is ratified by the Rajya Sabha.

Thus, from the above, we have seen that the Constitution has vested very strong powers in the Centre. Therefore K.C. Wheare, describes it quasi federal in nature.[iii]

Cooperative Federalism

With the passage of time, however the concept of competitive federalism slowly gave way to cooperative federalism. This trend has been promoted by three powerful factors:

1. The exigencies of war when for national survival, national effort takes precedence over fine points of Centre- State division of powers.

2. Technological advances mean making of communication faster.

3. The emergence of the concept of a social welfare state in response to public demand for various social services involving huge outlays which the governments of the units could not meet by themselves out of their own resources.

The concept of cooperative federalism helps the federal system, with its divided jurisdiction, to act in unison, it minimizes friction and promote co-operation among the various constituent governments of the federal union so that they can pool their resources to achieve certain desired national goals. Money has been one of the strongest motive forces in the emergence of this concept. The center with its vast financial capacity is always in a position to help the units which always need it to meet the expanding demands on them for social services following int their legislative spare, and this brings the two levels of government closer.[iv]

It means that though there is a constitutional provision for the distribution of powers in practice, these powers are to be exercised jointly by the center and states. As observed by distinguished jurist M.P. Jain, these governments are interdependent and not independent.[v] Though there is division of functions between the center and the units in a federation, and the respective areas of competence of each is earmarked, as these governments act side by side in the same country, inevitably many types of relations arise amongst them.

From Competitive to Co-operative Federalism

In the three older federations of the U.S.A., Canada and Australia, in the formative stages of development, the dominant operative concept was that of 'competitive federalism' which denoted a spirit of competition and rivalry between the Centre and the States. With the passage of time, however, the concept of 'competitive federalism' slowly gave way to 'cooperative federalism'. This trend has been promoted by three powerful factors:

1. The exigencies of war when there is a threaten to national security then center takes over states.

2. Technological advances mean making of communication faster.

It has come to be realized that the various governments in a federation are interdependent and they work in co-ordination so as to promote and maximize public welfare.[vi]

The framers of the Indian Constitution took due note of the emerging trend of co-operative federalism in the older federations. They realized that government in a federation were arranged not hierarchically or vertically but horizontally, that no line of command runs from the Centre to the States, and that common policies among the various governments can be promoted not by dictation but by a process of discussion, agreement and compromise. Several features and provisions of the Constitution have been deliberately designed to institutionalize the concept of Centre – State co-operation.

The provisions for enabling Parliament to legislate in the State area on the request of two or more States, the scheme of financial relations between the Centre and the States, grants-in-aid under Art.282, the scheme of Centre-State administrative relationship along with provision for all-India services, are some of the instruments to promote inter-governmental co-operation and introduce the necessary flexibility in rigid federal set up.[vii]

Legal Framework for Cooperative Federalism

Art. 1 of the Constitution of India states that India, that is Bharat, shall be a Union of States. Thereby implying no unit constituting the Indian Union can secede from it, the country is divided into several units, known as States or Union territories. The Union of India is a federal Union with a distribution of powers, of which the judiciary is the interpreter.[viii]

Art. 261 provides full faith and credit clause to be given throughout the territory of India to public acts, records and judicial proceedings of the union and the states. The term public acts in this article refer not only to statues but to all executive and legislative acts. The clause however docs not envisage that a greater effect to be given to a public act of one state in another state than it is entitled to the home state itself. Hence, ultra vires or unconstitutional statute need not be recognized in any other state.

Under entry 12, list III, 'recognition of laws, public acts and records and judicial proceedings' is a concurrent subject. Therefore, the states are also entitled to legislate on this matter but subject to the exclusive power conferred on parliament under Art. 261(2).

Under Art. 261(3), a final judgement or order delivered or passed by a civil court in any part of India is capable of execution anywhere within India according to Law. This is a constitutional provision that a decree shall be executable in any part of the territory of India according to law. The clause applies to civil and not to criminal courts.[ix]

Art 263 provides that the president may by order appoint an Inter-State Council if it appears to him that public interest would be served by its establishment. To create strong institutional framework to support the cooperative federalism in India. It may be charged with the duty of:

a. Inquiring into and advising upon disputes which may have arisen between states.

b. Making recommendations upon any subject and, in particular, recommendations for the better co-ordination of policy and action with respect to that subject.

It appears from the above that the council is envisaged to be an advisory body having no authority to give a binding decision. The council's function to inquire and advise upon Inter state disputes is complimentary to the Supreme Court's jurisdiction under Art. 131 to decide a legal controversy between the governments. Under Art. 263, four regional councils have been set up for making recommendations for the better co-ordination of policy and action with respect to sales tax, a state subject. A regional council has been established in each of the four zones – Northern, Eastern, western and Southern. A study team of the Administrative Reforms Commission suggested the establishment of an Inter-state Council under Art. 263 with a view to strengthen co-operation and co-ordination, and evolution of common policies, among the Central and State Governments in many areas where the measures taken by these governments from time to time are mutually interactive.[x]

Institutional Framework: NITI AAYOG

The Aayog, which has taken over from the old planning commission, is promoting a bottom-up approach to development planning. NITI Aayog performs following functions which help in achieving cooperative federalism.

1. The institution has to provide government at the central and state levels with relevant strategic and technical advice.

2. The infusion of new policy ideas and specific issue-based support.

3. To respond to the changing and more integrated world that India is part of.

NITI Aayog will function in close Cooperation, Consultation and Coordination with the Ministries of the Central Government and State Government. It will provide critical directional and strategic input to the development process, focus on deliverables and outcomes. [xi]

<u>**Conclusion**</u>

The Scheme of distribution of powers, representation of states in law-making and policy making and the establishment of bodies like Inter- State Council, Zonal Councils, the Governing Council of the NITI Aayog all demonstrate the conviction of the government to develop a unified framework of cooperative federalism.

The Sarkaria Commission and Punchhi Commission on Centre – State relations gave several recommendations to cultivate cooperative federalism and suggested actionable steps. Certain constitutional amendments can better federalism and its actualization to list a few –

- The office of the governor should be a political, and the terms of his removal should be altered and therefore the appointments of governor should be strictly non-partisan.
- Restricting the use of president's rule under Article 356 to prevent excessive misuse by the center.
- Extending the mandate of the Inter-State Council beyond advice and recommendations.
- The other dimension of tension in our federal system has been the demand to create new states. In December 1953, the state's reorganization commission was set up and it recommended the creation of linguistic states.

When there is a dispute between state and center over autonomy and other issues like the share in revenue resources, then judiciary acts as the arbitration mechanism on disputes of legal nature. Ultimately, the people and the political process must develop a culture and a set of values and virtues like mutual trust, toleration and a spirit of cooperation. A responsive polity sensitive to diversities and to the demands for autonomy can alone be the basis of a cooperative federation.